More Tales from
Hog Heaven

Nate Allen

www.SportsPublishingLLC.com

ISBN: 1-58261-710-4

© 2004 by Nate Allen

Interior photos: Courtesy of Arkansas Media Relations

Publisher: Peter L. Bannon
Senior managing editor: Susan M. Moyer
Acquisitions editor: Scott Rauguth
Developmental editor: Doug Hoepker
Art director: K. Jeffrey Higgerson
Dust jacket design: Heidi Norsen
Project manager: Alicia Wentworth
Imaging: Kerri Baker and Chrisine Mohrbacher
Photo editor: Erin Linden-Levy
Vice president of sales and marketing: Kevin King
Media and promotions managers: Monica Heckman (regional),
    Randy Fouts (national), Maurey Williamson (print)

Printed in the United States of America

Sports Publishing L.L.C.
804 North Neil Street
Champaign, IL 61820

Phone: 1-877-424-2665
Fax: 217-363-2073
Web site: www.SportsPublishingLLC.com

This book is dedicated to my beloved wife Nancy.

You inspired, prodded and cajoled me to write Tales from Hog Heaven *and somehow you did it again to get me to complete* More Tales from Hog Heaven.

Just another reason that I will love you until the 12th of Never and Beyond.

Contents

Part One

Football

Kiss and Tell

Louis Schaufele lettered for John Barnhill's Razorbacks in 1948 and '49 and Otis Douglas's Hogs in 1950, but it was as a football official that he earned election to the Arkansas Sports Hall of Fame in 2003.

It wasn't until late in Arkansas's Southwest Conference tenure, after repeated Arkansas protests, that officials with any geographical or past college ties to Arkansas were allowed to officiate games involving the Razorbacks. That chafed Arkansas, because the otherwise all-Texas-based league put no restrictions on Texas-born officials working games involving the Texas-based schools.

Baylor coach Grant Teaff wasn't keen at all about the new idea of an Arkansas-based official refereeing an Arkansas game, especially when he saw Schaufle plant a quick kiss on a Razorback cheerleader at the homecoming game in Fayetteville.

"Grant came up asking, 'What's all this about?,'" Schauefele recalled at his Hall of Fame acceptance speech in Little Rock. "But then he understood. I explained, 'That cheerleader with the alumni cheerleaders is the mother of my grandkids, and I want to keep her on my good side.'"

An Official Recount

Schaufele recalled officiating Colorado versus Notre Dame in the Orange Bowl.

"There was a timeout," Schauefele said, "and one of the officials came up to me and asked, 'How many people you suppose are here?' And I said, 'Oh, I guess the stadium holds about 75,000.' And he asks, 'And how many you think are watching on television?'

"And I said, 'I don't know, maybe 25 million.'"

"And he asks, 'I wonder how many of those people know your fly is unzipped?'"

Easygoing Otis

Joe Dugan and Jack Bailey both were at the University of Arkansas during the end of the John Barnhill era in 1949 and the beginning of the ill-fated Otis Douglas era of 1950.

"Otis Douglas really was ahead of his time," Bailey said, "but what he should have done was run some of us off, then he would have had a football team."

Dugan agreed.

"I remember," Dugan said, "one of his comments was, 'If you guys can put up with what we put you [through] in practice, I don't care what you do the rest of the day or what you drink.' And they took him up on it."

Not the Big Dance

Barnhill before him and certainly Bowden Wyatt after him were considerably firmer with their players than was Otis Douglas.

"I remember one practice for John Barnhill," Jack Bailey said, "and I was running the ball and kind of tiptoed around trying to see if I could find me another hole. He stopped practice right there and said, 'I'm not teaching any damned ballet class!' It was embarrassing, but he made his point."

Fayetteville Via Wyoming

Bobby Proctor went to Northwest Mississippi Junior College and got the attention of Wyoming coach Bowden Wyatt. Wyatt had old buddies in Mississippi who told him about Proctor.

So Proctor was Wyoming bound. Or so he thought.

"I was hitchhiking to Memphis," Proctor said, and a woman in the car says, 'Where do you go to school?'

"And I said, 'The University of Wyoming.' She said, 'You don't have a coach?' And I said, 'What do you mean?' And she said, 'He just went to the University of Arkansas.' And I said, 'Oh, my God! That's where I always wanted to go!'

"I called Coach Wyatt and he said, 'Let me see what dogs will hunt, if you know what I mean, and I'll get back with you.'"

Apparently the dogs took their time on the recruiting trail.

"January came and went," Proctor said. "February, March. It's April and I'm playing tennis, and this Cadillac drives up and I said, 'Oh, my God!' [Wyatt] gets out and says, 'You want to come?' That was it. I didn't sign anything. Oh, he did ask me how much I weighed. I said, '160.' He said get on the scales. The needle wavered at around 150. He said, 'You'd better start eating cornbread and beans or you're not going to last."

He almost didn't.

"When I got here," Proctor said, "we had six teams and I wasn't even on a team. So I was seventh team when we had six. Somebody got hurt at wingback, and I got to practice a little bit. We run a play and Eddie Bradford hits me and my nose is bleeding everywhere. We go back to the huddle and Bowden says, 'Are you hurt?' and I say, 'Shit, no!' The next play I get hit from the other side. I thought, 'I need to get away from these damned guys.'"

But he didn't get away and he did last, lettering for Wyatt's first Razorback squad that survived a Junction Boys' setting to go 3-7. As a senior in 1954, Proctor captained the fabled Southwest Conference championship Razorbacks of 1954 that went 8-3 and were dubbed "The 25 Little Pigs" by *Arkansas Gazette* sports editor Orville Henry.

Hedging a Sting Operation

As blunt as they come according to those who played for him, Bowden Wyatt did hedge at least once, Proctor said, on a matter concerning Razorback Charles Faulkinberry.

"I remember Bowden getting so mad at Faulkinberry after a play in practice," Proctor said. "He shoves him and he goes right into a hedge and there are wasps in there and he lights out of there, and Bowden says, 'Faulkinberry, get back in the huddle. That's as fast as I've ever seen you move!'"

Under the Table

Bob Hines, a Razorback from Illinois in the early 1960s, recalled an under-the-table dealing with Barry Switzer. Switzer was a Razorback graduate assistant on the prowl when he came into a bar that was supposed to be off limits to players.

Hines and his date were already seated at a table.

"I figured Switzer was looking for babes rather than to catch players," Hines said, "but I knew if he happened to spot me, I was in bad trouble. So I hid under the table. Only problem, a girl at the next table over lost her purse. So she's down crawling around looking for it, sees me down there and screams and jumps up.

Hines continued.

"There's all this commotion," Hines said. "I look up and see Switzer grinning like a Cheshire cat. But he still doesn't see me. He's just grinning 'cause he's figuring something interesting is going on. I stayed under the table until he had gone. About five years later I told Switzer. Until then, he never did know what happened."

Now What?

Seldom have so many celebrated so little about recovering a national championship-preserving fumble. However, quarterback Freddie Marshall and his 1964 Razorback offensive teammates weren't thinking about recovering a national championship with the fumble they recovered against Baylor. They were just trying to recover oxygen.

Marshall set the stage.

"We weren't a big-play team in '64," Marshall said. "It took us about a week and a half to score on each drive. It was like four yards, three yards, five yards, two yards, and then one of those long passes for seven yards. That's how our offense operated. Mistake-free, but not real exciting."

So nothing seems unusual how his Baylor story started back in '64 at Little Rock.

"We get the ball against Baylor on our 20," Marshall said, "and do one of our patented drives that takes up about three and a half quarters."

Then Broyles surprised everyone except Baylor's Bobby Maples.

"We're down at the 2," Marshall said, "and for God's sake I don't know why, Broyles called this play—he called for a pass. Bobby Maples, their All-America linebacker, reads my mind and intercepts the pass on the goal line. And he doesn't have anything but 100 yards straight ahead of him. Well, our offense had just gone about 15 plays and we're totally exhausted, and now we have to turn around and sprint to catch Maples. At about the 50, Maples starts running out of gas and he starts looking for somebody to lateral it to. One of our players happens to hit him and he fumbles and we recover, probably at about our 30."

The 11-0 national champions of 1964.

Marshall didn't name the Razorback who recovered. Probably because the spent teammates—if they had the energy—would have been more inclined to slug him in the jaw than pat him on the back.

"Nobody could say anything," Marshall said. "We're totally exhausted. Well, Broyles had preached for years and years about character. I can't do his Georgia accent, but he'd always say, 'Boys, you've got to have character!'

"Well, here we are in the huddle. We've just run a 70-yard dash and we're sucking wind. Jerry Jones is bent over in the huddle and he can't breathe. I thought he was going to die. But I thought we were all going to die as well as him. He looks up and says it like Frank, 'Boys, if we can take it in from here, we've got character!' So we all look at each other and say we've got to take it in. Another 14-play drive, and we get the touchdown. We had the ball 28 snaps and it took a quarter and a half, but Baylor never got to touch the ball."

Driving Through Cotton

The drive for which Marshall is most remembered took a trailing Arkansas team 80 yards in nine plays during the fourth quarter to beat Nebraska, 10-7 in the 1964 Cotton Bowl. The win capped an 11-0 season.

"We got the ball with eight minutes left," Marshall recalled. "So for 52 minutes, neither team could move the chains. We were playing between the 30s. Nobody could make a first down and they punted to us. ...Bill Pace (Arkansas's offensive coordinator) had noticed when I would sprint out right or left that the defense would rotate pretty heavily that way and it left the backside unprotected. We threw a couple of throwback passes, and then Jim Lindsey made an incredible catch of a pass he never saw because I threw it early. In that drive, I think I threw five passes and completed five, ran the ball three times and then the last play Bobby Burnett scored from the three. I had fumbled the ball once, thrown for an interception once, and I didn't know whether Broyles was going to put me in for that last drive or not. But he did. So I went from goat to hero because I won the most valuable player of the game award just on that one drive."

In between Baylor and Nebraska was an epic 14-13 victory over Texas, though the incident Marshall remembered most occurred in a 17-0 victory at Texas A&M.

"A&M had an All-America defensive tackle, and we're playing in College Station late in the third quarter," Marshall said. "It was a close game, must have been 7-0 at the time. I break the huddle and call the play. We did a lot of audibles, and their 12th man, the crowd, is so loud that our players can't hear. So I bring them back to the huddle. We line up again and they did it again, and I look over at Coach Broyles and he said, 'Don't run it.'

"We walk back. We did that four or five times. After the fifth time (offensive tackle) Jerry Welch says, 'Freddie, for God's sake please snap the ball this time.' And I said, 'Why?' And he says their All-America tackle said, 'If you don't snap it the next time, I'm going to jump across the line of scrimmage and whip your ass!'

"We had a lot of that kind of stuff that year. What I remember about that team is not so much the highlights but the character and integrity and the leadership of the seniors on that team.

"We get together a lot."

Pick a Quarterback, Any Quarterback

M aybe what bonded that '64 team was the adversity and disappointment of promises gone unfulfilled in '63. Broyles's 1963 Razorbacks followed 9-2, 8-3, 8-3, 9-2 seasons by skidding to 5-5.

After three years of Billy Moore quarterbacking, Broyles had as much trouble deciding who should succeed the departed All-American as the Hogs were having winning games.

"In '63, I started three games," Marshall said. "Billy Gray (the Razorbacks' longtime associate athletic director) started three or four games, Jon Brittenum started three games. What we had was a pitching rotation. And if you walked a batter, you got taken out. That wasn't conducive to getting the team confident in a quarterback. To this day Broyles admits he made a mistake in '63 in not settling on a quarterback. I'm not saying it should have been me, though I certainly felt like it should have been, and I told him that after the eighth game of my junior year."

He told him a lot more.

"I told Broyles I'd practice as hard as I could the next two games," Marshall said, "but I was almost complete with my academic work and I could finish early and that I wasn't coming back the next year. The next to the last game against SMU he called me off the bench in the second quarter, and then he started me against Texas Tech and then he called me into his office after the season and said, 'You will be my quarterback.'"

That lasted one game but happened again.

"I got hurt the first game of '64 against Oklahoma State," Marshall said, "and Billy Gray came in and won the game, and I didn't play at all in the Tulsa game, and then I started the TCU game and I started every game after that, and he moved Gray to defense and redshirted Brittenum. He told me he would go with me come hell or high water."

Marshall's quarterbacking days didn't end at Arkansas, but they never were the same.

"I played in the Canadian League at Calgary," Marshall said, noting he rejoined a couple of UA alums. "Wayne Harris was up there at the time, and Jesse Branch was up there a couple of years. But I got hurt and decided professional football wasn't the way I was going to make a living. I learned I was never going to be anybody's No. 1 quarterback in the NFL. I thought I could go up there, get a couple of years' experience and go to the NFL, but I got hurt and decided, 'No, I'll do something else.'"

Back in Fayetteville last September for his induction into the UA Sports Hall of Honor, Marshall got a laugh during his speech describing hell-raising Billy Moore's recruiting influence upon him in choosing Arkansas over LSU.

"Billy Moore," Marshall said, "thank you for taking me to the Sigma Chi Gold Rush party. Because I was on my way to LSU until my visit here. When Billy took me to the Sigma Chi Gold Rush party. I thought, 'If that's what college football and college life is about, this is where I want to be.'"

A Smart Man Belies Low Grades

Lynn Garner was an All-America linebacker but something of an academic joke while lettering for Frank Broyles's Razorbacks from 1967-69.

"I majored in P.E.," Garner said at the Spring 2003 Lettermen's Reunion. "And that don't stand for Petroleum Engineering."

Razorback Foundation vice-president Harold Horton, who coached Garner in 1968 and '69 as the linebackers coach, joked, "Lynn, we want to show you the new Academic Center so you can finally see what one looks like."

They laughed at the jokes, but nobody laughs at Lynn. When the Valdez spilled oil in the 1980s, they didn't call a Chancellor's Scholar. They called good, old boy Lynn Garner and his Garner Environmental Services, the largest environmental cleanup company in the U.S., Garner said.

"We worked in New York," Garner said of helping clean up the 9/11 aftermath. "And we did the Valdez. The Valdez wasn't all that bad. Just a lot of it. The worst oil spill we had to work was one in Houston where we had a bunch of floods and a bunch of pipelines burst, and there was black oil, and diesel and gasoline and they all caught on fire.

"An Admiral from Washington flew in and was sitting there saying, 'My God! Is there anything we can do?'

"I said, 'Yeah. I'm probably going to need another cash register.' He didn't like that at all. They are kind of like wives—the sense of humor goes out."

Actually, Lynn's wife, Sharon, helped him get the last laugh. Lynn was a high school football coach in the Houston area when he figured he needed to get into another line of work as his wife wanted to attend law school.

"Coaches have to move around," Garner said. "So I was going to have to quit that if I was going to be with her while she was in law school. She talked to an old boy who was running a company in town that cleaned up oil spills. I went to work as a salesman, and two or three years later started my own deal. Now we're the biggest and the baddest."

A Wife by Assignment

"My wife and I met while I was coaching Cy-Fair High School down in Houston," Garner said of his wife, Sharon. "She was teaching school and flunking all these football players. I was defensive coordinator, and the head coach said, 'You need to meet this Sharon and get some of these guys passed.' We started dating and I got 'em passed. He didn't give me a raise, though. I'm still a little pissed off. Actually, he and I are still good friends."

School of Hard Knocks

Garner's success might shock the academic pointy-heads but wouldn't shock anybody who played football for the coaches Garner played for, the late Bill Stancil at Fort Smith Northside, and then the late Wilson Matthews, his linebacker coach his first two years at Arkansas, before finishing under Harold Horton.

"I was scared of Coach Stancil," Garner said. "He and Wilson Matthews were two peas in a pod. Coach Stancil would wear Bermuda shorts with a cutoff T-shirt and a whistle. He had huge love handles, and he'd wear a jockey strap over them and he had a clipboard nailed to another board. He'd hit more guys and break helmets off you... oh... but I loved him. He was a good guy who died a few years ago."

Matthews died in 2003 but lives on in every Razorback he ever met.

"The most hell I ever went through was going through spring ball my freshman year," said Garner. "[Matthews would] kill you. He beat the snot out of you. They had a bunch of telephone poles they used in drills, and those poor guys we practiced form tackling on... We'd hit them and knock them into the telephone poles."

The only thing worse for the scout team fodder than taking a dive so their bell wouldn't be rung quite as hard by the telephone poles was to run so well that the first-teamer missed the tackle.

"If they did it too well," Garner said, "they'd have to do it again."

Garner actually played his best ball under Horton when he and Cliff Powell both were All-America in 1969, but he couldn't resist gigging his old coach after Horton had teased him about seeing an academic center for the first time.

"Shoot, Harold didn't have to coach," Garner said, laughing with Horton in earshot. "He just had great players. With me, Cliff Powell and Guy Parker, he didn't have to do anything. We made him."

No doubt they helped make Horton's reputation, which Harold enhanced in becoming an Arkansas Hall of Fame member with two national championships coaching the University of Central Arkansas.

Sleepless in New Orleans

Garner recounted his favorite party story, involving himself and his roommate, Guy Parker, which occurred two nights before the '68 Hogs beat Georgia, 16-2 in the Sugar Bowl at New Orleans.

"A bunch of girls were having a party, and the team had a bed check," Garner said. "We waited for the coaches to come around and did all that, and then we said, 'Let's go.' We start out and there is Coach Broyles sitting in a chair in the middle of the hall reading a paper. It was like Laurel and Hardy. I stopped and Parker runs right over me and we fall out. And Coach Broyles says, 'Get back in there!'

"So we go back in the room and these girls are calling, saying, 'We've heard so much about you two.'"

So much for curfew.

"To make a long story short," Garner said, "we tied our bedspreads on the balcony. We were on the eighth floor, and on the seventh was a parking lot. There was an overhang and we climbed to it and jumped down and stayed out all night. We had locked the door so the coaches couldn't get back in to check on us. So for us to get back in the next day we had to swing back in through the balcony."

It was the most exercise they were fit for that day.

"We hadn't been to bed," Garner said, "and we're supposed to be watching film: offense on one side and defense on the other. Richard Williamson (receivers coach) comes up and starts chewing us. We had whiskey, puke, everything on us, still drunk as a skunk.

"I get down there and the defense is all snickering because the only seats are in the front row. And Parker hadn't shown up. All of a sudden they turn the lights on to switch the reels and Guy comes in and says, 'Shit! I've been sitting in the wrong one over on offense.' He's still drunk and stumbling, and all the guys are laughing. Then we practice, and Parker starts throwing up in the defensive huddle.

"Charley Coffey (the defensive coordinator) and Coach Horton, they are all just mad. But then I had a great game. Georgia was undefeated and No. 2 in the nation. They got a safety on us and were going into the end zone, and I hit the runner and caused a fumble to go through the end zone and we got the ball back. So they didn't get on me for much."

Of course that gave Garner something to celebrate New Year's night.

"That night we were on Bourbon Street," Garner said. "And I'm with Gary Parson, who is about 6-8 or 6-9. There was a carload of girls driving down Bourbon Street and we stop and talk to them and this cop hits me with a nightstick and says, 'You are blocking traffic. Get out of the way!' Parson didn't even know he had hit him with that deal and raised up, and the cop looks up at him and says real nice, 'Oh, you all mind moving? You are blocking traffic.' Me, he had whopped and said, 'You're going to jail, boy.' Meanwhile, (assistant coaches) Don Breaux and Richard Williamson are watching across the street laughing at us."

Who, Me?

Before becoming a fixture at the insurance industry's million-dollar roundtable, Stuttgart-born John Eichler learned first-hand about policies for the unexpected. Only instead of selling insurance, Eichler was the insurance as the sophomore reserve quarterback for Frank Broyles's Razorbacks against Oklahoma State in the 1967 season opener.

"I was the third-string quarterback and had never taken a snap with the varsity at all," Eichler recalled. "Ronny South was the starter, and Gordon Norwood, who had been All-Everything in high school, was second string.

"We were behind 7-6 in the fourth quarter against Oklahoma State, and I'm sitting on the bench with my helmet off looking in the stands, not even paying attention. I hear someone holler, 'Eichler!' And I think it's somebody in the stands hollering at me. Then I hear 'Eichler' hollered again, and I look up and Coach Broyles is up motioning. I thought maybe he might want a Coke or something. I almost went up there without my helmet. But I go up there with my helmet on and say, 'Yes, sir.' And he says, 'Right 68 X curl' and slaps me on the butt and throws me out [on the field] in front of 50,000 people.

Basically it was a fake off tackle and keep the ball, and I did and ran 37 yards up the sideline.

"My first play as a Razorback. The crowd is going wild, the clock is running down. I keep a couple of more times and we're down on the 4-yard line. Not until a couple of years ago did it even dawn on me that, gosh, we could have kicked a field goal and won right there. But he called another off tackle play. I go to the left and I'm keeping the ball, and as I go to the goal line a guy tackles me and his helmet hits the ball and knocks it out, and they are laying on top of me and I can see the ball bouncing and people diving for it, and Oklahoma State recovers and we get beat."

Sneaking to Fame

With the Hogs going south with South the following week in a 14-12 loss to Tulsa, Broyles announced the next day that Eichler would start the SWC opener against TCU. Paced by Eichler's incredible touchdown on a 76-yard quarterback sneak, Arkansas won 26-0. The 76-yard sneak brought Eichler recognition from Arkansas clear back to the Big Apple.

"I had people write me from New York," Eichler said, "that said they saw it go across the ticker at Times Square, and I got a letter on stationery from the John Eichler Brewing Company in New York. The Holiday Inn marquee in Fayetteville and Springdale said 'Happiness is Eichler.' So you could see the fans really wanted to win a game. It was pretty neat. For a week I could hear the whispers and heads turn and little kids wanting my autograph."

Eichler described the sneak turned 76-yard TD.

"I think it was just before halftime," Eichler said. "(Offensive line coach) Merv Johnson gave the signals from the sideline. A signal like this, both hands around the nose, was a quarterback sneak. We were on the north end headed south on our 24-yard line. I followed the center with my head down and I got hit by the middle linebacker. As I started to go down, I pushed myself back up trying to get a little bit more, and as I did, I never saw another defensive man. The defensive halfbacks and safeties all blitzed and all came running in. So I just went that direction. And I just ran. As I circled the end zone, I saw Frank Broyles standing there with his arms outstretched and he hugged my neck. That may be the last time he hugged my neck."

Probably was. Eichler logged only two more starts without a win that 4-5-1 season.

"The next game was Baylor," Eichler said, "and we had to make a drive and kick a field goal in the rain to tie it (10-10). And then came Texas (a 21-12 loss). I like to say I had a great completion ratio that day. Not many balls hit the ground. Only problem was, Texas caught four of them. I really thought they caught five, but the record book showed four. They put Ronny back in and he almost pulled it out."

Divine Intervention

Mike Bender would coach at Arkansas four different times under three different head coaches and be a standout tackle on Arkansas's 1964 national championship team. But first he had to be recruited from Strong—with a little help from the Scriptures—to play for Frank Broyles's Razorbacks.

"Back then you could sign conference letters of intent," Bender said, "that weren't binding until the actual signing day. I had signed with Oklahoma State because Arkansas only offered me a one-year scholarship. Jim McKenzie (the Razorbacks' defensive coordinator) sat down with my mother and daddy and said, 'Son, where have you always wanted to go to school?' I said, 'I've always wanted to be a Razorback.' He said, 'Why are you going to mess up and even think about going somewhere else?' And I said, 'I don't know.'"

Then Mckenzie played his trump card.

"Coach McKenzie knew my mother was real religious," Bender said. "He asked my mother to get the Bible out. He read a couple of verses and my mother said, 'It's time to eat. And Mikey, you are going to Arkansas, aren't you?' As soon as we finished eating, he called Oklahoma State on his credit card, stuck the phone at me, and I told them I wasn't coming."

Talked Too Much

Mike Bender coached perhaps the best group of Razorback freshmen never to play a freshman game back when the UA still had freshman teams. The '73 varsity was so thin that such freshmen, who later became NFL players, like R.C. Thielemann, Greg Koch, Dennis Winston and Gerald Skinner played for Broyles instead of freshman coach Bender.

"Coach Broyles started talking to me about some of my boys," Bender said. "I started bragging on them and the next thing I knew he was taking them up. I should have kept my mouth shut."

We've Got Your Back

In 1995, Bender coached the Razorback offensive line for Danny Ford.

"Danny wanted you to substitute people," Bender said. "I've never been very good at substituting offensive linemen that much unless you get ahead. I figured they were first team for a reason. But he was getting on to me. We're getting ready to play South Carolina, and he says, 'Bender, when are you going to put the second bunch in?' I said, 'Coach, third series I'm going to throw them out there.' He said, 'They had better go in!' Third series we're backed up on the minus 1, and I send them in. And he meets me and says, 'What are you doing?!' I said, 'Coach, I'm sending them in.' He said, What!?' I said, 'Coach, you said, send them in, and they are going in.' They went in and drove that booger 99 yards. You talk about a relief ... I thanked the Lord up above because Danny was fixing to get me."

Jumping Their Case

As a coach, Bender patterned himself after Merv Johnson, the quietly effective coach who coached Bender during Mike's Razorback offensive linemen days. Occasionally, though, Bender could come out smoking like the legendary Wilson Matthews in his fiery prime.

Russell Brown, a redshirt freshman starting guard in 1995, got lit up by Bender.

"I remember jumping Russell so bad," Bender said. "He was a freshman and he's starting. He's thinking he's the big horse on campus and he goes out in a Thursday practice and flops around and looks like a junior high guy. I had never fussed at anybody like that. I chewed it up one side and down the other and tried to humiliate him. I went on and on. At the end of that season Russell said, 'The only man I ever let talk to me like you did that day is my Daddy. And you talked to me worse than my Daddy did.'"

Brown, Grant Garrett and Brandon Burlsworth were the line's Three Musketeers offensive linemen. They were together every day of their five-year college careers, which culminated in a 9-3 SEC West co-championship season under Houston Nutt in 1998. However because of their individual makeups, blue-collar everymen Brown and Garrett would get the bristly side of

Bender more than the so-earnestly-eager-to-please Burlsworth did.

"Russell one day said, 'Coach, you never fuss at Burls like you do the rest of us in these meetings.'" Bender recalled. "And I said, 'Russell, Burls is special.'"

The whole team knew that even before mourning the walk-on who became an All-American. Burlsworth was killed in an automobile accident in the spring of 1999, shortly after being drafted by the Indianapolis Colts.

A Razorback Defects

Bobby Roper played for Frank Broyles's 1964 national champion Razorbacks, but his last active football game in Fayetteville was against the Razorbacks, not for them. Ken Hatfield, one of Roper's 1964 Razorback teammates, was in his first year as Arkansas's coach in 1984 when Roper came calling with Texas A&M as part of Jackie Sherrill's Aggie staff.

Looking at Texas A&M and Arkansas as they warmed up that cold, rainy November 17 in Razorback Stadium, the runty Razorbacks looked as meager as the weather. The muscular Aggies filled their football suits like vintage Miami, Southern California and Oklahoma teams inevitably do.

But A&M unraveled like cheap toilet paper in the cold rain. The runts routed the Aggies, 28-0. Roper took it personally. Still does.

"I had been back to Arkansas one time since I graduated," Roper said. "So it was real important to me. It had been in the 70s all week at College Station and everyone is running around in shorts. We get up here and it felt like 20 below. We weren't prepared for that. We went in the tank early—like when we got out of the dressing room. We got hammered. That was one of the most disappointing times. I really wanted us to play well, and we played like horse manure."

A Step Back in Time

The historic Crescent Hotel in Eureka Springs felt prehistoric to Bobby Roper during his Razorback playing days.

"We used to stay at the Crescent in Eureka Springs the night before Fayetteville games," Roper said. "We'd go over a bridge they sometimes wouldn't trust. You had to get off the bus. They'd drive the starters and the best backups across and then you'd walk across. I walked in '63. I never will forget that elevator up there. It had a door that pulled across the elevator that would kind of unfold. It was 1961, but that looked like it came out of the 1700s."

The entertainment was more modern, though still 40 years behind the times, Roper said.

"We didn't have TVs in the room," Roper said. "We had a radio and a bunch of books that were all published in like 1920. You had 60 guys between 18 and 20 years old, and the biggest entertainment was to go out on the porch and listen to the crickets."

He even had a beef about dinner.

"They always served you a steak," Roper said. "You'd take a bite of it and start chewing it and it started swelling on you. That steak would last for a week."

Mazzanti Sees Red

His Southwest Conference debut made Jerry Mazzanti see Red. And that is Red with a Capital R.

"We played against TCU when TCU had Bob Lilly (an eventual NFL Hall of Fame defensive tackle) and they may have had another All-American, too," recalled Mazzanti, a lineman from Lake Village who lettered for Frank Broyles's Hogs from 1960-62. "I was on the second unit, and you had to play both ways. TCU had a lot of big tackles. Red Henderson was our offensive tackle on the other side. Red jumped offsides, and it caused the tackle on my nose to come across the line. He hit me and rolled me over on my behind. Our quarterback looks down and says, 'Jerry, what are you doing back here?' I got up cussing Red Henderson because I wasn't about to cuss that big tackle from TCU."

Reppond on a Roll

Razorback fans in the early-'70s portion of the Frank Broyles era recall Mike Reppond as a record-breaking receiver, but there were two spring practices the Joplin, Missouri native was tried at defensive back.

"I intercepted a pass right off the bat and thought I was a stud duck," Reppond said. "Until the next scrimmage—that's when Russ Garber broke into the open."

Garber was a fullback from the old school.

"He was so tough he refused to wear a mouthpiece," Reppond said. "One time in practice I saw him spitting out teeth. He came back to the huddle a bloody mess. (Offensive backfield coach) Don Breaux said, 'Damn! What happened to you?'

"'Nothin'. Run the play.'"

Sounds like one to avoid tackling unless you've got a S.W.A.T team for backup.

"Yeah," Reppond said. "But I had intercepted that pass the last scrimmage and I thought I could take him on. He rolled me up like wallpaper. I wanted to get the license of the truck that hit me. A play like that makes you pick up the pieces. Only it was me they were picking up."

Was Reppond ever hit that hard again?

"No," Reppond replied. "But (Southern California linebacker) Richard Wood came close. I caught a pass over the middle, and he hit me so hard my ancestors felt it."

Watts Up?

As much as Arkansas fans griped about "Texas refs" in the otherwise all-Texas based Southwest Conference, they griped most about the officiating against a Southeastern Conference team. It was against Tennessee in the Liberty Bowl of 1971, some 21 years before Arkansas joined the SEC. And it made referee Preston Watts that year's most hated man in Arkansas.

Arkansas offensive lineman Tom Reed recovered a fumble by Razorback halfback Jon Richardson, handed the ball to an official, then saw Watts hand the ball to Tennessee.

Also, a Watts holding call on Razorback tight end Bobby Nichols voided Bill McClard's field goal that would have given Arkansas a 16-7 lead and thus the game.

Arkansas lost, 14-13.

"That was something that to this day I don't understand," Reed said of the fumble. "Equally as bad was the holding call on Bobby Nichols, the tight end, on the field goal. The same official, Preston Watts, made both calls. I don't know what he saw. But he called holding, and you watch the film and there is obviously no hold. And on the fumble recovery he was towards the middle of the field making the call right off the bat that it was Tennessee's ball."

The middle of the field was not the middle of the action, where Reed recovered Richardson's fumble.

"It was a screen pass to Jon Richardson on the Tennessee sideline," Reed recalled, "and I had been in front of him on a block when the ball fell out. I didn't even have to move. I just fell on it. And there was an official there, and that official even questioned Mr. Watts as to why it was Tennessee's ball. I went straight to him (Watts). I don't remember what I said, but he informed me not to say anything else and keep my mouth closed or we would be penalized. I had handed the ball to the closest official. He took it from me and went to Watts and said the Arkansas player has the ball, and Watts acted like he didn't even hear him. It was Tennessee's ball."

Reed shook his head.

"The fumble was more obvious because everyone could see it," Reed said. "But the holding call was equally bad. There was no hold.

"On film you see the Tennessee guy look up to see if the kick's good, and it is good, and you see him put his head down and start walking off the field. If he had been held or something else, he would have been jumping up and down screaming. It was crazy. I don't understand what happened. But it did happen, and you can't do anything about it. You don't understand how something like that could happen on any level, much less college. I thought about it and thought about it. There wouldn't be a day that I wouldn't think about it for a long time after that. And I still will go back and think about it at times.

"We were a better football team than Tennessee and outplayed them in every aspect."

Lon's Tricks of the Trade

Before going into administration as the dawn to midnight assistant athletic director, the late Dr. Lon Farrell was one of the best and cleverest recruiters on Frank Broyles' football staff.

To recruit Rolland Fuchs, a key running back on Arkansas's 1975 Southwest Conference championship team, Lon arrived at the Fuchs's Kansas City home unshaven, rumpled, looking exhausted. Lon apologized but said he had recruited in Colorado the previous day and had driven all night just so he could see Fuchs on time that morning.

Actually Farrell spent the previous night in a Kansas City hotel. He slept in rumpled clothes and didn't shave just to appear like he drove through exhaustion to see Rolland Fuchs no matter what.

Better Bank on Tradition

Tom Rystrom, a Kansas City, Kansas, native and the last player to start at quarterback for Frank Broyles, also was Lon Farrell's last recruit before fully moving into the administration side of athletics. Rystrom knew he was going to sign with Arkansas, but decided to have a little fun at the earnest Arkansas assistant's expense. So shortly before the signing date when Farrell called, Rystrom recalled saying, "Well, Coach, I like Arkansas. But, gee, Kansas State offered me a horse and a horse trailer."

Lon didn't miss a beat.

"Well, Tom," Farrell reasoned according to Rystrom, "that trailer will rust, and that horse will get old and die, but the Razorback tradition will live on."

Rystrom remembers sighing a resigned sigh.

"Where do I sign, Coach?" Rystrom said. "How can you not sign after that?"

Truly Generous

Farrell oversaw the spring sports, among other things, so former spend-happy swimming coach Sam Freas always was butting heads with Lon over expenses, recruiting trips etc. However, Freas became one of Lon's staunchest admirers.

Brian Finnerty, one of Sam's British imports who never worked out as a major swimmer, had long completed his eligibility but was still hanging around Fayetteville when he became stricken with colitis.

"Brian Finnerty is broke and he's sick," Freas told Farrell. "He can't get home, he looks like he's at death's door and he doesn't have the money to see a doctor. What can we do?"

Freas paused.

"Dr. Lon took care of it," Freas said of the assistant AD with a Ph.D. "He paid for Brian's medical bills out of his own pocket. We always think how tight he is with the university's money, but old Dr. Lon is quite a guy."

He was that. All who knew him still mourn that the man who helped so many couldn't help himself through the severe depression that caused him to take his own life.

Put 'Em Up

Lon was an outstanding all-round athlete in Pittsburg, Kansas—especially as a boxer. He boxed while in the service and did quite well, he recalled, save at least for one particular fight.

"One guy hit me so hard," Farrell said, "it spun me around. My back was to him, and I was boxing and jabbing at nobody in front of me."

The referee stopped the fight lest Lon continue shadow boxing the ring post. At least Lon stayed on his feet long enough to be TKO'ed instead of counted out. A pretty good feat, that. The guy who knocked him silly, Harold Johnson, later became light heavyweight champion of the world.

Banquet Humor

Lon had a favorite story that he would tell at banquets. It involved a young monk sworn only to say two words every five years.

After the first five years, the Monsignor asked, "Well it's been five years. What have you got to say for yourself?"

"Food bad," the young monk replied.

After the next five years, the monk was asked what he had to say.

"Bed hard," he replied.

The third five years passed and he again was asked to utter whatever two words he choose.

"I quit," he said.

"Doesn't surprise me," the Monsignor said. "All you've done is bitch since you've been here."

Snow Job

Defensive coordinator Monte Kiffin snowed the Razorback defense he inherited after he joined Lou Holtz's first Arkansas staff in 1977.

"I remember Coach Kiffin," said Jimmy Walker, a Razorback All-America defensive tackle lettering from 1975-78. "When we were out practicing, it was snowing in Fayetteville. We were out there freezing and really wanting practice to be over. And Coach Kiffin said, 'It's not cold out here!' He ripped his shirt off and jumped over the pile. We thought this guy is crazy. But it showed us, if this guy can stay out here with no shirt on, surely we can stay out here with our pads on. He always told us, 'It's a mind thing. If your brain tells your body it's freezing out here, you'll freeze.' So I've used it on my wife. I'll say, 'It's not cold out here. Just don't tell yourself it's cold.'"

Did it work?

"She thinks I'm crazy," Walker said.

Going South

During Frank Broyles's 1958-76 Razorback coaching tenure, some Razorback invetiably would mimick Broyles's trademark Georgia accent. Quarterback Ronny South apparently did a good Broyles impression during Johnny Majors's tenure as a Razorback assistant coach.

"We're out at practice," Majors recalled at the 2004 spring Razorback Reunion. "And Ronny South yelled, 'Everybody in!' And he sounded like Frank. I said, 'Okay,' and took off running to the locker room. Well, Frank hadn't released us. So he had pulled my chain."

Looking Away

"When Ronny redshirted (and was on the offensive scout team), I coached the defensive backs," Majors said. "My last year I coached the offensive backs, and quarterbacks, and Ronny and John Eichler were the quarterbacks. I always taught the defensive backs to keep their eye on the quarterback, that the quarterback's eyes will tell you where he's going to throw the ball. Of course Ronny knew this. So I'm coaching quarterbacks and we're practicing in goal line and Ronny takes the ball out and pitches without even looking. I said, 'Don't you ever do it again.'"

Better Head North

Majors so liked it at Arkansas that he didn't instantly leap at his first head coaching chance.

"Johnny Majors got offered the Iowa State job," Broyles said, "and couldn't decide whether to take it. So I came up to him and said, 'Johnny, you're fired.'

"And he said, 'I'd better take the job, hadn't I?'

"I was joking, but I meant it, because I knew it was a great opportunity. He wasn't there for two years before he went on to Pittsburgh and won the national championship."

Addressing the Razorback Reunion, Majors teased that Broyles's motive at the time might not have been entirely altruistic.

"Coach, you just didn't want to pay me the recruiting bonus ..." Majors said. "The last year before I left for Iowa State I recruited Lynn Garner, Dick Bumpas, Bill Montgomery and Chuck Dicus."

All four made somebody's All-America team. Dicus is in the College Football Hall of Fame.

"I didn't always recruit like that," Majors said. "That was my best year recruiting as an assistant."

Saving Face

Earl Campbell always beat Arkansas, but Texas's great running back from 1974-77 never beat Arkansas defensive end Johnnie Meadors (1973-76).

"I was at a birthday party last weekend," Meadors said two springs ago, "and the subject of the University of Texas came up. I mentioned Earl Campbell, and someone turns and says, 'The last time I saw Earl, he was dragging you down the field.' I said, 'Oh, I don't know what game you were at, because the last time

I saw Earl, he was slammed in the opposite direction by me. He dragged a few, but not me.'"

Meadors smiled. Big Earl would have dragged him, too—except Johnnie cheated.

"In the years I played against Earl," Meadors said, "I never allowed him to turn the corner on me. We played in Austin my senior year, and Earl actually was getting ready to turn the corner on me. Well, I grabbed him by the face mask and said, 'Not today, Earl. Not in your lifetime are you going to turn the corner on me. I'll take a 15-yard penalty first.' And that's what I did. They flagged me, but I said, 'You aren't going to turn the corner on me.'"

Above Board and Above Ground

Johnnie Meadors had an outstanding Razorback career including starring at defensive end for Frank Broyles's final Southwest Conference championship team that closed the 1975 regular season clobbering unbeaten, prohibitively favored Texas A&M, 31-6 in December at Little Rock and then whipped Georgia, 31-10 in the Cotton Bowl.

But Johnnie may have never stood taller than in 1995 when his little nephew, five-foot-four J.J. Meadors, caught Barry Lunney's low touchdown pass in Tuscaloosa to beat Alabama, 20-19.

'Bama fans yelped the pass wasn't above ground and thus not above board.

"The one they say that was fumbled—that it hit the ground, that it was incomplete...that was a completed pass," said Johnnie. "As short as J.J. is, it can't get to the ground first."

Thanks, Earl

Thanks to Earl Campbell, Arkansas never beat Texas from 1974-77, yet thanks to the great Texas running back, Frank Broyles's 1975 Razorbacks won a tri-share of the Southwest Conference and beat Georgia in the Cotton Bowl. With Oklahoma battling Texas to recruit the Tyler Rose out of Tyler, Texas in 1974, Arkansas was able to steal off with Ike Forte, the transfer running back from Tyler Junior College who led the Razorbacks in rushing both in '74 in '75.

Forte, a native of Texarkana, Texas signed with Barry Switzer's OU Sooners out of high school, but needed two years at Tyler to become academically eligible for NCAA Division I.

"I was down there at Tyler," Forte said, "and Barry Switzer came down to Tyler and somehow it got into the press that he had told Earl, 'Earl, you need to come up here. We haven't signed a quality back yet!' Well, I took that personal. And he had a flock of running backs already."

Arkansas recruiting coordinator Leroy Montgomery certainly emphasized all that.

"Leroy Montgomery kept after me even after I signed with Oklahoma," Forte said. "I told Leroy I'm coming, and then the next thing I know I'm on Highway 71 (in January as a Tyler graduate transferring at semester) going up the mountain and it started snowing. I thought, 'Where am I going?' I had made only one other trip up there when I flew up for a visit."

Did he think he was coming to the wrong place as the snow mounted?

"I thought about that," Forte said, "but I kept going. I wound up at Barnhill (the site of all athletic offices then), pulled up in the front, and they were waiting on me, and the rest was history. I loved it."

Three Questions for Thumper

Razorback fan Jim Watson relayed this story as told to him by former Razorback trainer Jim Bone. Bone first was an assistant trainer to the late Bill "Groundy" Ferrell under coach Frank Broyles.

For maybe the only time of his career, All-America Razorback linebacker Wayne "Thumper" Harris had staggered dazed to the sideline, his bell rung.

"Groundy always had three questions he'd ask somebody whose bell had been rung," Watson said he was told by Bone. "'What's your name?' 'Who are we playing?' 'What's the score?' So as Wayne wobbles off, Groundy comes up to ask the questions with Frank coming in saying, 'Tell Groundy your name is Wayne Harris. We're playing Baylor and we're behind, 7-0! Now get your ass back out there!'"

Everyone at Arkansas, especially his old linebackers coach, the late Wilson Matthews, referred to Harris as "Thumper." The nickname accompanied him to college from his high school days in El Dorado.

"My 10th grade year," Harris said, "I made a hit and one of my coaches said, 'You can hear that thump up in the nickel seats.' That's where the Thumper came from and it followed me to Arkansas."

Matthews once recalled a Thumper thump that knocked out SMU quarterback Don Meredith: "It is hard to see a receiver when your eyeballs are in the back of your head."

It's a shame that Matthews died just before Harris's long overdue 2004 induction into the College Football Hall of Fame. Already in the Canadian Football League Hall of Fame, the State of Arkansas Hall of Fame and the University of Arkansas Sports Hall of Honor, Harris was elected to the College Hall of Fame on April 6, 2004 and will be inducted on December 7, 2004.

According to Matthews, who coached some great ones including All-Americans Ronnie Caveness, Cliff Powell, Lynn

Garner and Ronnie Mac Smith, Harris was the best he ever coached.

"Football has changed so," Matthews told this writer several years ago. "I don't know if you can compare athletes [from different decades] since they are so much bigger and stronger and faster right now. But I still say Wayne Harris was the best at his position up here that I had any knowledge of. And it wasn't just here. He proved it in Canada. He was never hurt. He was so quick. He played linebacker, but he could have played anywhere. In today's football he would be a great free safety, where they play those guys like linebackers a lot. Against Rice he intercepted a pass 35 yards deep."

Wrong Way to Stardom

Harris—5-11, 185—did everything wrong to come out so right.

"It was unreal," Matthews said. "You'd coach like hell to keep people from running around blocks. Because if you are running around blocks, you are chasing. You are not going to make the play. But he'd jump around the damn blocks and make plays. It was uncanny—his feeling for where the ball was and how he would get to it. And when he got to you, it wasn't no damned arm-tackling. He'd pop your ass."

Barring More Info

Just hours before the streaker butted his way into Razorback history at the October 26, 2002 homecoming game with Ole Miss, Neal Galloway shared additional information about a story of a nude Razorback dancer back in the 1980s. Galloway was a reserve Razorback center from Stuttgart for Lou Holtz from 1979-82. He had read an anecdote in the first *Tales from Hog Heaven* concerning the exotic dancer at Wilson Sharp Athletic Dormitory.

The dancer, "a big old lineman with a bag on his head," according to former Razorback Mike Ihrie, danced nude in a strobe-lighted window as fans were filing by from the Broyles Complex parking lot to Barnhill Arena for a basketball game, while another Razorback football player, Randy Wessinger, worked the crowd beckoning, "Come one, come all. See the exotic nude dancer of Wilson Sharp!"

Reading the anecdote, Galloway laughed about the dancer he publicly referred to only as "Nasty."

"I'd forgotten all about that," Galloway said. "The exotic dancer, we like to say that he had some dates with my mother."

Say what? Neal laughed and explained.

"Willie Nelson had a concert one football weekend," Galloway said, "and my parents came up with two or three couples. Not all of them liked the concert, my dad being one of them. So he went back to the hotel and Nasty was kind of my mama's escort for the evening. We always had a time about Mama and Nasty dating. So when I got hold of your book, I said, 'Well, Mama, you had a date with an exotic dancer.'"

Neal was asked for his flashbacks concerning the night of the "Unknown Dancer."

"I don't know if Nasty and Ihrie were rooming together," Galloway said. "I wasn't on the same floor with them. I didn't know what was going on, but I could hear Wessinger down there, and I noticed people looking, and I couldn't figure out what it was all about. I remember we checked it out and just died laughing. I couldn't believe that."

Wished He'd Bit His Tounge

God forbid you ask Holtz the wrong question at the wrong time.

"Even as a kid," Galloway said, "I knew how stupid it was five minutes after I did it. But during my junior year, when they had me alternating some with Jay Bequette, I think Lou sometimes would create a controversy between first and second teamers. So we went through one week where Lou was saying he didn't know who he was going to start. We were playing Texas Tech out in Lubbock. My parents went to all the home games, but Lubbock was a long way. They said, 'Now if you think you are going to start, we'll go.'

"I tried to catch Lou coming off the field. What I messed up was that a couple of reporters were around. So you can imagine what happened when I asked, 'Coach, do you know who you are going to start?' He said, 'Boy, don't come up here asking me that! You ought to consider yourself lucky that you are just making the trip! And you want to know if you are going to start?'

"It was just a big scene. I felt like trying to crawl under the turf. But…he was a whole different person later. He saw me in the Broyles Complex and explained everything and said, 'Don't let it bother you. You are doing well.'"

One-Trick Pony

Galloway said Holtz was a brilliant coach and motivator, but the brilliance could wear thin with the older players.

"He could motivate," Galloway said, "but he was kind of a one-trick pony once you had been around for awhile. I remember my junior year going into a meeting before a game thinking, 'Either it's going to be we don't deserve to be here, or we are the best team ever to have suited up. Which are we supposed to be this week?'"

No More Overtime

Galloway says he can't fathom how Holtz has adjusted to the NCAA rule limiting practice and meetings to a maximum 20 hours a week.

"If we had that rule when I played," Galloway said. "We would have had to shut [practice for the week] down by Wednesday morning."

Baby Doc

Derek "Doc" Holloway of Palmyra, N.J. played for Holtz as one of the smallest wide receivers ever to be a Razorback. This did not help Galloway when he arrived as a walk-on center.

"We walked in for our weight test," Galloway said. "I wasn't benching 250. Doc Holloway got 225 and popped it about 10 times fast. I thought, 'These little-bitty receivers lifting like this, this is not going to be pretty.' I thought, 'I might have gone in way over my head if our little, itty-bitty receivers are this strong.' Luckily, you found out not many guys were as strong as he was."

Heartbreak Hotel

Before he became the Razorbacks' All-America placekicker in 1981, Bruce Lahay impacted Arkansas as an Elvis impersonator. Or rather, Arkansas impacted his Elvis impersonation upon him.

It was the last Orange Bowl practice in Fayetteville before the 1977 Razorbacks upset Oklahoma, and Lahay, a quarterback in high school as well as a kicker, was in the scout team backfield impersonating Elvis.

But not Elvis Presley, of course.

"The last play before we went to the Orange Bowl," Lahay said. "I was Elvis Peacock (OU's other great wishbone halfback along with Billy Sims). I dragged to the line of scrimmage and drug across the middle of the field and caught a screen pass that went for about 15 yards. Monte Kiffin (the defensive coordinator) just exploded. 'Defense, get over here!' He says, 'Mr. Lahay, I want you to catch the ball right here. And he turns to (vicious-hitting linebackers) Larry Jackson and Mike Massey and says, 'If Mr. Lahay catches the ball beyond this point, we are going to be here until midnight!' 'Oh, no,' I thought. I drag to the line of scrimmage and I count one thousand one, one thousand two and I'm thinking, 'This one is going to be okay, too.' Just as I catch the ball, the lights went out. Kiffin comes running over, cheering the defense, all fired up. I get up, kind of staggering over to the huddle, and he pats me on the helmet and says, 'Are you okay?' I raise up my hand and it's already swollen. And he says, 'Don't worry, this is the last play.' He takes me into the training room (to trainer Dean Weber) and says, 'Weber, fix Lahay's hand.'

"I wouldn't give those years up for anything."

Haven't the Foggiest

Recruited out of St. Louis by the outgoing Frank Broyles staff, Bruce Lahay didn't have the foggiest notion what he was getting into visiting Arkansas the day athletic director Broyles named his own successor as football coach.

"I flew down here on a Friday in December," Lahay said, "and that was the weekend Lou Holtz signed with Arkansas. They had him at Barnhill Arena, and they introduced him at halftime as the new head football coach. It was so foggy, I didn't see any of the stadium or anything. Dense, dense fog. We couldn't land at Drake Field, and I had to fly to Fort Smith and then drive up to get it here. There were four or five schools, Missouri, Illinois, Indiana and Michigan State, that put heavy recruitment on me. I visited Indiana, Michigan State and Missouri and Arkansas. When I got back after my visit from Arkansas, by Thursday the next week I probably had 200 letters from fans of the University of Arkansas. 'Welcome to our family. Our house is your house. You'll love it down here.' I didn't get that from any of the other schools. I thought, 'Man, if these people are that fanatical about football, I think this is the place I should go.'"

A Lefthanded Compliment

Lahay was a lefthanded quarterback in his St. Louis prep days but never quarterbacked at Arkansas, other than his 1977 season on the scout team and in junior varsity games.

"When I first came," Lahay said, "it was my choice to play quarterback. Turned out not to be the head coach's choice. My sophomore year Lou told me, 'You know I really don't like lefthanded quarterbacks.' So I became a kicker full time."

Right after Steve Little exited an All-American in 1977, Arkansas had three great kickers from 1978-80 in Lahay, Ish Ordonez and Steve Cox. In '78 while Cox redshirted as a transfer from Tulsa, Lahay punted and Ordonez placekicked.

In '79, Ordonez kicked PATs and medium to short field goals, Cox kicked off, attempted long field goals and long punts, and Lahay pooch-punted, always pinpointing them well inside the 20, and held for placekicks. Lahay redshirted and practiced placekicking in '80 while Ordonez and Cox divvied the chores up as seniors.

Any one of them could have been an All-American like Lahay was when he had the show to himself in 1981. Yet the trio remains the fastest of friends.

"I still talk to those guys," Cox, a banker in Jonesboro, said a while back. "Ish is in L.A., and Bruce is up there in Northwest

Quarterback Kevin Scanlon had to quickly learn the rules under new coach Lou Holtz during an 11-1 1977 season.

Arkansas. The day there was the shooting at the school in Jonesboro, both Ish and Bruce called me up to check on my kids. That's just the kind of guys they are. We were all competing against each other, and 20 years later they are calling to check on my kids."

Breaking Lou's Rules

Though he couldn't play as a redshirting transfer, quarterback Kevin Scanlon knew Lou Holtz better than any Razorback on Lou's first Arkansas team in 1977 that went 11-1 and beat Oklahoma in the Orange Bowl.

Scanlon had quarterbacked for Holtz at North Carolina State in 1975 and '76. So after Scanlon backed up senior incumbent Ron Calcagni in 1978, Holtz gave latitude to Scanlon—as the senior starter on Arkansas's 10-2 1979 Southwest Conference championship team—that he never gave any other Arkansas quarterback.

Of course, the wide latitude was still often accompanied by Holtz's scathing standards.

"Holtz had a bunch of rules for quarterbacks," Scanlon recalled. "'Don't pitch the ball under duress, don't force the ball in a crowd, don't change the play to get to a better play, just get out of a bad play.' There were all these rules and he would ask you them all the time, in the hall, on the bus, in the locker room. Particularly the young quarterbacks. 'What are the rules?,' and you'd have to repeat them. We're down 17-0 to Baylor. I had thrown three interceptions for the first eight games, and I'd already thrown three in the first half against Baylor. They were killing us. Holtz calls me up in front of the whole team. 'Scanlon, get up here!' He grabs me by the shirt in front of the whole sideline and goes, 'Do you know those rules?'

"And I'm like, 'Now? You want me to tell them now?! Yeah, I know the rules.' And he says, 'Well, forget every [damn] one of them.' He said, 'You take chances and do whatever it takes.'

"And I said, 'Okay,' and we came back and won, 29-20. I think he felt he needed to relax me and relax the team, and it was, 'Just go have fun and do what it takes.'"

Breaking a Pattern

"In the same game," Scanlon recalled, "it's 20-20 with three minutes left. A pattern Holtz had was there would be a hard-fought first down late in the game, the other team would think we're driving towards a field goal. And as soon as we got the first down, he'd throw the out and up. We had hit Texas Tech and Texas A&M with it the previous years. So we get the first down at the 40, and I'm thinking we're running the out and up, and a couple of linemen are saying the same thing. But he sends in a running play, and I'm thinking we're going to grind it out and kick a field goal. Second and six he calls the out and up, and we hit it to (Robert) Farrell for a touchdown. I'm coming off the sideline, and I said, 'Coach, I thought you were going to call that out and up on first down.' And he looks at me and says, 'Don't you think they might be thinking that, too?' He knew we had a pattern and wanted to break it."

Lou Improvises

Watching endless film, Holtz had his game plans more rehearsed than a Broadway play. Yet he could, and would, ad-lib something off the wall like a kid drawing plays in the dirt at a sandlot game.

The '79 Hogs turned what would have been a devastating tie with perpetual Southwest Conference underdog TCU into a

16-13 victory at Fort Worth with one of Lou's fourth-quarter concoctions.

"It's 13-13," Scanlon said, "and Holtz says, 'We're going to run an out and up to the tight end (Darryl Mason). But I want you to pump it to Mason and go deep to him. We don't have this play, but we're going to put it in right now.' I said, 'Coach Holtz is the blocking the same?' He said, 'Yeah.' And I said, 'Who is blocking the backside end?' And he looks right at me and said, 'You are.' I said, 'What?' And he's laughing and says, 'Nobody is blocking him. Get the ball off the quick. You can do that.' I said, 'Okay,' and we hit it for 50 yards and end up kicking a field goal with 10 seconds left to win the game."

Right Out of Raleigh

Scanlon remembers Holtz improvising in the '79 team's 17-14 victory over Texas in Little Rock.

"It's third down and 11," Scanlon said, "and we call time-out and he says, 'You know what will work right here? A middle screen to the tight end.' I said, 'Coach, we don't have a middle screen to the tight end.' He said, 'Yeah, we do.' He starts describing the play, and I said, 'Coach, we ran that at N.C. State. We've never run that here.' He says, 'You know the play. Go out and tell the linemen to do the same thing, tell the tight end to slip over the middle. It's going to work.' I told them and they said, 'What?' But we hit it for 10 3/4 yards, and the next play I snuck for a first down, and then Gary Anderson took a pitch for our first score."

Scanlon Calls Plays

"The Alabama game," Scanlon said of the Sugar Bowl loss to the 1979 national champion, "we're fourth and four on the four, and he says, 'What do you want to run?' And I say, 'I want to run a slant.' And he'd say go run it. He let me call some major plays, like the two-point play against Baylor that Farrell made the great catch on. After that year, I said, 'Coach, what was the difference? My junior year you never listened to me. My senior year you are letting me call plays.' He said, 'Kevin, you were the difference. Your junior year you would say, 'I think we need to run this. Your senior year you said, 'We need to run this.' I knew whatever I called that you wouldn't have as much confidence in what I called as what you called.' But his first answer was, 'You were a senior. And if it didn't work, I was going to blame it on you.'"

In Your Dreams

Scanlon said everyone on the 1977 team remembered there was a long delay before the kickoff against Oklahoma on New Year's Night in Miami, and that Holtz had asked players to tell some jokes or a story to ease the tension. A player dreamed up a different way to break the ice before the Hogs met national champion Alabama two bowls later.

"We're playing Alabama in the Sugar Bowl," Scanlon said, "and there's a pregame delay and we're in the dressing room and he says to the team, 'Is there anything you want to say?' And (senior linebacker) Mike Massey says, 'I do.' He said, 'Coach, last night I had a dream, and in the dream I was on the kickoff team and I hit the guy and he fumbled, and we went in and scored.' And there's dead silence. And Coach says, 'Well, Mike, there's one problem. You aren't on the kickoff team.' But we kick off and they fumble and we recover against the No. 1 team in the nation before 80,000 on national TV. Of course we're not expecting to have the ball, so I say to Coach Holtz, 'What do you want to run?' And he says, 'I don't know, let's ask Massey.'"

An All-Conference Demotion

As Arkansas was readying in Fayetteville for the Sugar Bowl, Scanlon was named the SWC's Offensive Player of the Year. Holtz told the squad about it before practice and led the applause for Scanlon, then in practice proceeded to berate the quarterback like Sergeant Snorkel dressing down Beetle Bailey.

"Tom Jones!" Scanlon remembers Holtz shouting to the redshirt freshman backup quarterback. "Get in there! Scanlon, get your ass on the scout team!"

Scanlon recalled going bewildered to the other end of the field where the scout team offense was simulating Alabama against defensive coordinator Monte Kiffin's starters.

"You just now getting here?" Kiffin said, smiling. "I was expecting you 20 minutes ago."

Scanlon recalled saying, "'Huh? You mean this was planned?' And Kiffin said, 'Oh, yeah. He told us at lunch he was going to do this. You didn't stand a chance.' Coach Holtz knew about that award and was sending me a reminder. Nothing is bigger than the team."

Freshmen Fiascos

Freshman football games used to be a fairly big deal before freshmen became eligible for varsity football participation in 1972. Then freshmen football games began devolving into games merely with freshmen not precocious enough to help the varsity. So the so-called freshman teams began to get rounded out with veteran scout-teamers far more familiar with running someone else's offense and defense than they were with whatever their own team was operating.

All of Arkansas's best freshmen were helping Arkansas tie Houston for the SWC championship in 1979 when the remaining freshmen and some scout-team lifers got waxed "something like 55-0" in a junior varsity game at Misouri, Charlie Fiss recalled.

A longtime Cotton Bowl executive, Fiss was a student assistant in the Razorbacks' sports information office for that long trek up and back to Columbia, Missouri.

"We had to punt a lot," Fiss said. "And our punter got hurt. So Kent Reber, a defensive back, had to punt by the end. He kicked it straight up in the air and it bounced backwards, something like minus-14 yards. I remember (defensive tackle) Earl Buckingham, one of the few good players we had, standing on the sideline watching us fumble and asking, "Are they charging admission for this imitation of a football game?"

Buckingham's sardonic wit would get topped.

"On the way back home," Fiss recalled. "Some gigantic bird crashed into the bus's windshield. Mike Bender, one of the coaches, glanced up and said, "That's the best lick I've heard all day."

Vintage Orson

Orson Weems lettered on Lou Holtz's offensive lines from 1981-83. During Orson Weems's Arkansas era, the late Orson Welles was in the farewell toast of his acting career and did TV commercials about Paul Masson wines never being rushed prematurely to sale. So, Orson Weems adopted and adapted Orson Welles's Paul Masson slogan as inspiration never to be offside.

Said the Razorback Orson: "We will block no line before it's time."

A Frustrating Tie

After a controversial pass interference penalty enabled SMU to tie Arkansas, 17-17 in 1982 and knock Arkansas out of the Cotton Bowl picture, a plaids-and-stripes-clashing clad reporter asked Razorback All-America defensive end Billy Ray Smith if it was "a frustrating tie."

"No," Billy Ray reportedly said before gently grasping the reporter's necktie, "but this, this is a frustrating tie!"

The reporter, a former softball teammate of Smith, insisted Billy Ray actually said, "That's a nice tie."

That may well have been true, but in the legend's aftermath, Billy Ray knew tying it up with "frustrating tie" made for a good story and he's sticking to it.

A Swimming British Bobbie Kicks for Lou

Martin Smith has Razorback distinctions no one can match. He is and always will be the only English bobbie to be an All-American and Olympic swimmer who placekicked barefoot for Lou Holtz and then coached the Razorback swimmers until men's swimming was dropped from the program.

Smith, who had played soccer in England, walked on as a kicker after completing his Razorback swimming eligibility for coach Sam Freas. Freas, the P.T. Barnum of swimming, was one of a kind, but so was Holtz, Smith said, in a completely different way.

"He was a commodity I never experienced," Smith said. "Very much a control guy. It was almost like everyone out there was afraid of him. They were afraid of messing up. No one would stand up to him if they felt like he was wrong. I had never been around something like that. The sports I was involved with there was give and take, and you could talk to your coach."

Martin described his first scrimmage kick as one of Lou's one-way conversations.

"It was the first big scrimmage with referees," Smith said. "A pretty big deal. I was kicking off for one team and Bobby Hahn for the other. We were out there getting ready to kick off, and (assistant coach) Sam Goodwin said, 'Onside kick.' I said, 'Okay.' I only knew one onside kick and that was overload left. So we get out in the huddle and I call, 'Onside kick, overload left.' The referee blows the whistle and I shout, 'Ready,' and the whole team shifts to the left. All of a sudden I hear, 'Hold it! Hold it! Who the hell called that play? Who the hell called that play?' I raise my hand, 'It was me.' 'Get the hell out of there! Get the hell out of there! Get me another kicker that knows something about football!' I went over to Sam Goodwin and he just shrugged. He wanted a surprise onside kick. How the hell did I know what a surprise onside kick was? We had never worked on it."

Nobody crossed Lou regardless of circumstances.

"I always wondered," Smith said, "how a little-bitty guy could grab a big, old lineman by the face mask and pull him along like a Woody Hayes wannabe. So small and so frail. But those were good times. I wouldn't trade my days here for anything."

Marty Smith and the Net Loss

"Lou always called me Marty," said Smith, who always goes by Martin.

Imitating Holtz's self-confessed lisp, Smith continued: "'Marty Schmith. Hey, Marty! Can you handle it?' That was an interesting deal playing for Lou. He was very much an entertainer at his team meetings who got people motivated. The only thing I didn't like about kicking for Lou was he wouldn't let kickers use a kicking net warming up on the sideline. I used to ask Coach Holtz and Coach (Ken) Turner and they'd say, 'Hey, Ish Ordonez (the Hogs' placekicker from 1978-80) never had a kicking net. You don't need a kicking net.' I just never understood it. You wouldn't expect a golfer to sit for two and half hours and then go out and hit a drive without warming up. But the only time we got to use a net was the Bluebonnet Bowl (in '82 at the Astrodome in Houston) when we beat Florida. I remember one of the players saying, 'The only reason you've got a net is they want to impress the recruits that are here. How many kickers do you ever see in the NFL or Division I football that when they get in field goal position that kicker is over there kicking eight or 10 balls?'"

In '82, his lone season of football eligibility, Smith was a perfect 22 for 22 on PATs and kicked three of seven field goal tries, including a 27-yarder in the controversial 10-10 tie with SMU. He kicked four PATs in the 28-24 Bluebonnet Bowl victory over Florida.

"I didn't kick any field goals that game," Smith said, "but I always tell people, 'My four points won the game.'"

Not Suited to a Tee

Smith seldom kicked off in 1982, because the Hogs had a strong-legged walk-on named Bobby Hahn. Only trouble was Hahn used more tape than Linda Tripp to bound his kicking foot. Hahn's foot would be wrapped up like a mummy in such a way that he limped out to kick.

That exasperated Lou, particularly at practices when Hahn would still be taping when he was supposed to be kicking.

"The only times I kicked off," Smith said, "is when Holtz got mad at Bobby Hahn for whatever reason. Before the Rice game (in Fayetteville), Ken Turner told me, 'Be ready, because you are probably going to kick off.' I went to the equipment room because I used a different tee than Bobby Hahn did. It was one of those sideways tees which was a lot better for a barefooted kicker. But I went down there and there was no sideways tee. Bud Turk, the old equipment manager said, 'Use the same one we've got. That's what we've used for 20 years.' I said, 'I can't use that one.' He said, 'We don't have it.' I had to send my wife to buy one. This is how late it was. When we were running out on the field for pregame warmup, she threw it out on the field to me from the stands. After the game we went to a party at Dr. (Robert) McCollum's house. (Offensive line coach) Larry Beightol always went to Bob's parties. He heard the story and got so pissed off. He said, 'That's the most ridiculous story I've ever heard. I can't believe they didn't give you a tee.' But that's how it was for kickers back then. It was horrible."

How to Catch a Plane

Smith recalled talking with Holtz in Lou's Notre Dame days.

"I took our team up there to swim," Smith said, "and I went by there and spent about 25 or 30 minutes with him. He was doing really well at Notre Dame, and they were leaving that day because they were playing Air Force. He said, 'Well, Marty, I've got to go. Those planes are a lot easier to catch before they leave.' Everything was a one-liner."

Lou Saves a Life

Lou Holtz might have saved Byron "Bono" Yarborough's life one night. At least, he certainly saved the center he coached at Arkansas a long night of discomfort. When Holtz saved Bono, it was from one of many complications that turned a turf burn into near-death experience for the offensive lineman from Houston who was recruited by Holtz but actually did all his lettering for Ken Hatfield from 1984-86.

"I had a turf burn on my knee and it went downhill from there," Yarborough said. "I had sudomonis bacteria, and went through all sorts of surgeries and procedures and antibiotics, bowel sections, kidneys, lots of scars, staph infection, peritonitis ... I lost 70 pounds. I remember you interviewing me in the apartment and I was like a skeleton."

He was down considerably from the 300 he had weighed. Yarborough was ill and redshirted during 1983, Holtz's final Razorback season. He said Holtz, (former Razorback) Eddie Bradford, then in charge of the Northwest Arkansas Radiation Therapy Institute, and trainer Dean Weber visited him regularly and made sure his care was the best.

"One night in the hospital," Bono said. "Coach Holtz came in and checked on me and, I started crying and couldn't stop. I was hurting real bad. He went and found some poor resident and woke him up and went one up side of him and down the other. It turned out I had an abscess on my bladder and couldn't go to the bathroom. That's what hurt so bad. He checked on me all the time, and Mr. Bradford checked on me every day."

When Yarborough could play again, Hatfield was the coach.

"That's not one of those politically correct things to say," Yarborough said of comparing Holtz and Hatfield. "But I preferred Coach Holtz's ways as a coach and a person off the field. Coach Holtz was the one who recruited me and was here and then things change. Life changes. You look back on it, we were thinking, 'New coach ... what's going to happen? But you think in business that happens all the time. You get bought by another company, new owners, a new boss. So you don't realize it back then, but it's preparing you for life.'"

Nothing quite prepared Bono for driving into Fayetteville from Alliance, Nebraska, in the fall of 2002 to see the expand-

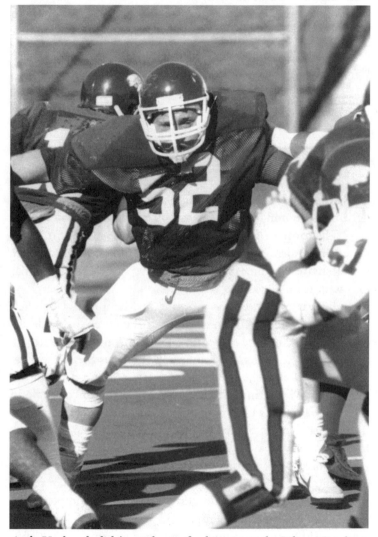

Andy Upchurch didn't much care for his trip to the Liberty Bowl in 1984. But he was all for Hogs first-year coach Ken Hatfield.

ed 72,000-seat state-of-the-art Reynolds Razorback Stadium replacing the tin can he remembered as Razorback Stadium.

"Coming over the hill on Cleveland Street," Yarborough said, "I started to see the stadium and I told my daughter, 'Daddy played football here.' And as I rolled over the hill, my jaw dropped. And I said, 'No, Daddy didn't play football here.' It's amazing! Awesome! Something else!"

Don't Give Me Liberty

Had Andy Upchurch been Patrick Henry, there would have been no pondering "Give me liberty or give me death."

The former Razorback center from 1981-85 wasn't much for Liberty, at least not the 1984 Liberty Bowl and its lack of, he said, festivities leading up to the game, especially on Christmas Day with team already reported.

"It was on Christmas morning in Memphis," Upchurch recalled, "and we were tired of eating at the hotel. So we decided to go out and get something to eat. Unbeknownst to us, being college students, the only thing open was Steak and Egg. It was David Bazzel, me, Brother Alexander and a couple of other guys. We go into Steak and Egg and the only people in there on Christmas Day are people you would expect. No family, just people with broken teeth smoking cigarettes. Really sad, to be honest with you. This poor lady, an older lady, who was nice as could be, was waiting on us. She's also washing the dishes in one of those industrial dishwashers with the side panels that go up and down. She raises it up before it completes the rinse cycle. Boiling hot water goes all over her and her face. She screams, slips on it and goes to the floor screaming, 'My eyes! My eyes!' Nobody in the place except us responded. They just kept smoking their cigarettes and drinking their coffee. The manager is over just running the cash register, and this lady is slipping all around on this tile floor screaming, 'My eyes!' And then screaming, 'My contacts! My contacts!' We helped her and as we left we kept saying, 'What were we thinking? Going out to eat thinking something would be open Christmas Day.'"

Christmas in a Box

The Liberty Bowl did reward members of that 1984 team with "Christmas in a Box."

"We all had this dinner," Upchurch said, "and after dinner they gave us these boxes. From previous bowl games we were expecting sweats or hats, some neat stuff. But we open these boxes and they had hair nets, barbecue sauce, pantyhose... They went to every almost-out-of-business drugstore and got everything they could get. Razor blades, not like Bics, just the old individual blades themselves. Afro Sheen. Mustard. We called it Christmas in a Box. ... Some of that stuff had a shelf life of 400 years."

Singing the Blues on Beale Street

Ah, well at least there was the great blues on Memphis's fabled Beale Street. Upchurch's look cast a sour note.

"We go to these functions on Beale Street," Upchurch said. "In fact a guy had spoken to us in Fayetteville about a place he had on Beale Street. We go down there and it's cold and they've bused us down there and dropped us off and we go to this restaurant with the two different teams. So after the dinner, the teams mingle and go down to see what's on Beale Street. Nothing is open. Nothing. It's freezing cold. We go back to the restaurant and they've locked us out. They say, 'We are closed! We are closed!' We are looking for little cubbyholes and the wind is gusting and the bus doesn't come for an hour."

Upchurch had a much better time bowling in '85 at the Holiday Bowl in San Diego with warm weather, warmer hospitality and the last bowl victory Arkansas would garner until Houston Nutt's 1999 Hogs beat Texas in the Cotton Bowl on New Year's Day, 2000.

Better Ken Than Lou

Bad as that Liberty Bowl trip was, capped by losing to Bo Jackson and Auburn, Upchurch said playing for Ken Hatfield in '84 beat the bejabbers out of being under Lou Holtz the previous years. Reaction of players who played for both Holtz and Hatfield tends to be decidedly for one over the other. Andy definitely is a Hatfield man.

"Night and day," Upchurch said. "I felt like Coach Hatfield really cared about us, and Coach Holtz was interested only in what you could do for him. Holtz did have you prepared for anything you could possibly face. Hatfield was not a guy who worked on the details—Holtz did. But Hatfield cared. He taught me more about life than I had learned the previous years. He was like Houston (Nutt), a coach you would want your kid to play for."

Holtz could prepare for some great upsets, like when the 1981 Razorbacks routed heavy favorite Texas, but he could also over-prepare. Upchurch recalled the heavy Thursday practice the 1983 Hogs waged just two days before losing to Ole Miss in Jackson.

"The defense was going to the dorm eating dinner and the offense was still on the field in full pads," Upchurch said. "You couldn't even see the ball—one of his turn the watch back deals. And we go down to Ole Miss and get beat. We were worn out. It was about a five-hour practice Thursday night in pads."

Keep Your Butt in Oklahoma

Kirk Botkin might have gone straight from Baytown, Texas, to the University of Oklahoma instead of the University of Arkansas. Both schools were recruiting the eventual Razorback All-SEC tight end in 1989.

"I might have gone to Oklahoma," Kirk said, "but my mom didn't like Barry Switzer. My mom is extremely religious. She won't even say 'butt,' much less something like 'ass.' And she was really into getting me an education more than me playing football. So Coach Switzer is sitting there on our couch and talks football, football, football and says 'butt' twice and finally says, 'Oh, yeah, he'll get an education.'

"So he leaves and my mom is going, 'No. No.'

"And then Coach Hatfield comes and he talks about education, education, education and finally says, 'Oh, yeah. He'll play football, too.'

"He leaves, and my mom says, 'Oh, yeah. I like him.'"

The Botkins didn't get to like Hatfield for long, though they would meet again.

Hatfield left after Botkin's redshirt freshman year of 1989. Kirk would play for three more head coaches—Jack Crowe, Joe Kines and Danny Ford—before finishing as a two-time All-SEC tight in 1993.

After four years playing in the NFL, Botkin coached for two of his old bosses—Hatfield for one year in his first college coaching job as a graduate assistant at Rice, and as a full-time assistant going on four years now for Crowe at Jacksonville State.

Practice's Greatest Hits

Many a Razorback's most memorable moment comes from a practice he remembers unconsciously. David Schell recalled when he was a gangly, 205-pound freshman nose guard desperately recruited out of New Mexico by Ken Hatfield's first Razorback staff in 1984, when they inherited few defensive lineman. Schell drew raves his first Razorback practice. Only problem was, Schell was fuzzy why they were raving.

"I'm sixth string and supposed to redshirt," Schell said. "We do the dive drill where they put the cones three yards apart. You start out with the top offensive player versus the top defensive player, and it goes right down to the bottom players and cycles all the way back around. I was the very last player in the defensive line. We had one more defensive player than we did offensive players. So when I cycle through, I suddenly am up against Marcus Elliott, an All-America candidate almost 300 pounds. We fire off on this drill. Marcus hits me and all four snaps on my face mask burst—just blow up. But I stopped Rock (fullback Marshall Foreman) in the hole. So everyone is all excited and pumped up, and the coaches are congratulating me. But it took me 15 minutes to realize where I was at. If it wasn't for reading the University of Arkansas Razorbacks on the press box, I wouldn't have known where I was."

Riley Meets His Maker

Until a bad back required his retirement, W.L. Riley, or Riley as everyone calls him, worked long and hard as the cigar-smoking custodian of the Broyles Athletic Complex. Even a heart attack didn't sideline him for long, though Riley had a moment of thinking he had met his maker.

Riley had just opened his eyes in filmy, post-surgery semi-consciousness when he saw a hazy vision of Frank Broyles looking down from above.

"I knew he thought he was God," remarked Riley wryly. "And I thought, 'Damn! Maybe he is!'"

That actually was Frank looking down from above. The Arkansas athletic director burst into the hospital as soon as he had heard of Riley's heart attack.

Riley's wife, Betty, once was rushed from the Broyles Complex to the hospital by a high-priced ambulance driver. She had come looking to deliver a message to her husband, couldn't find him, didn't feel well and suddenly fainted. Hours later, an out of breath Ken Hatfield found Riley at the Broyles Complex.

"I've been looking all over for you!" Hatfield told Riley. "I took your wife to the hospital, stayed there to see that she's okay and came back looking for you. Now get your butt over there!"

Grim Reaper

Between playing under Broyles at Arkansas in the early 1960s and serving as associate athletic director in the mid 1990s through 2000, Jesse Branch was a Razorback assistant coach under Broyles, Lou Holtz and Hatfield before becoming the head coach at Southwest Missouri State.

Branch survived some turbulent times. Once he was seen apparently lingering aimlessly in the Broyles Complex hallway.

"What are you doing, Jesse?" he was asked.

"I'm just standing here to make sure Riley doesn't take my name off the door," Branch replied.

During the periodic purges that rocked coaching staffs in the Broyles Complex, Riley took down the names of the deposed from the office doors and replaced them with their successors. Riley's grim reaper rep spread fast during Lou Holtz's last years of revolving staffs.

On his first day succeeding Holtz as Head Hog, Ken Hatfield greeted Riley with, "I hear you are the most feared man in the North 40."

Custodian George Bartz inherited Riley's reputation. All it takes is a loss or two for George to be eyed nervously if he walks by the coaches' offices with a screwdriver in hand.

Not Out of His Depth

After throwing three interceptions in a 38-16 loss at Ole Miss in 1999, Arkansas junior quarterback Clint Stoerner was asked in a media teleconference if he had the same "depth perception affliction" afflicting some talk show caller's wife.

The next game, Stoerner rallied the Hogs from a 24-14 deficit to post a 28-24 upset over nationally second-ranked Tennessee.

"My depth perception," Stoerner said laughing, "ain't nothing wrong with it this week. But it changes week to week, you know."

Beating Tennessee in Fayetteville and Texas in the Cotton Bowl that 1999 season rank as Stoerner's fondest memories, particularly the triumph over Tennessee.

Unbeaten Arkansas, then 8-0 in 1998, had unbeaten Tennessee down late in the fourth quarter at Knoxville. Stoerner's foot caught the back of right guard Brandon Burlsworth's leg, causing a freak fumble. Tennessee, going on to win the national championship, recovered and rallied at the last to win, 28-24, the same score Arkansas won by a year later.

"I tried to do the manly thing and take it and take it and take it for a year," Stoerner said of constantly being asked about the 1998 fumble. "So to have it end like this... that's big time. It makes it all that much better. We beat the No. 2 team in the country when nobody gave us a chance. During a timeout one of their linebackers said, 'You haven't fumbled yet like you did last year.' I said, 'I wondered how long it would take before you said that.' So when we ran out the clock, that was sweet."

Ditto, Nutt

Coach Houston Nutt felt likewise.

"How ironic for the score to be 28-24 in the University of Arkansas's favor," Nutt said. "That's sweet."

Especially when things were so sour the previous week with a loss at Ole Miss.

"I was disappointed in everything last week. Disappointed in myself, my staff, my players. But they went back to work," said Nutt. "You appreciate that they don't give up on you. This is something they will take [with them] forever."

One Great Play Gathers Moss

Those '99 Hogs indeed will never forget topping Tennessee.

"When I tell my grandkids," Arkansas rover Ontraia Moss said, "that I played football at the University of Arkansas, they know I won't be making it up. Because I recovered a fumble in the Tennessee game, and that game won't be forgotten."

The game's aftermath won't be forgotten by those who worked at the then-operating Brew Pub on Fayetteville's Dickson Street. For several days, the Brew Pub's exterior decor included an uprooted goal post. Wildly celebrating fans removed the goal post from Razorback Stadium and marched it to Dickson Street before propping it against the Brew Pub so revelers could walk underneath it.

The Coolest Customer

Just about the time Houston Nutt gets exasperated out of his gourd trying to see if his quarterback has a pulse, Matt Jones coolly does something so phenomenal as to leave the whole Razorback staff marveling in amazement. Nothing so epitomizes Jones's laid-back ability to lay out the biggest plays than his 2002 Miracle on Markham that moved the Razorbacks 80 yards in 30 seconds to upset LSU, 21-20 in Little Rock and win Arkansas the SEC West.

Nutt recalled it all in a 2003 address to the Tulsa Razorback Club.

"Picture this," Nutt said. "We have 80 yards to go and we have 38 seconds left. I go up to Matt, 'Matt!' 'Yes, sir (spoken sleepily deadpan).' 'There's 38 seconds left, we're in a two-minute mode here. I need a sense of urgency!' And he's kind of sitting like this (sprawled, with his head back) on the back of the bench. 'Matt, do you hear me? 'I got you, Coach. Everything is cool.' I send him on the field and I'm looking at a couple of coaches thinking, 'I don't know, y'all. He's only completed one pass all game.' But lo and behold, the first play he hits a long one to Richard Smith down the sideline. All of a sudden we've changed ends of the field. From our 20 to their 30. I give him a play and another one, and it's third down and I give the signal for a triple post X drag. He's kind of halfway looking at me and I'm screaming, 'Look at me, man!' He calls the right play and throws this marvelous pass that had to be sent from the heavens above, and DeCori (Birmingham) catches it in front of three Tiger defenders. And I look at Matt and say, 'Unbelievable!' And he just says, 'Everything is okay, Coach.' Just as cool as he can be."

Jones quarterbacked the Hogs to a 9-5 mark and the West title in 2002 and a 9-4 record and an Independence Bowl victory over Missouri in 2003. He's also Arkansas's lone returning regular offensive starter for 2004 and the most exceptional big-play man of the Houston Nutt era.

Need a big play in a big game? "No problem," says the always-cool Hogs QB Matt Jones.

In the bowl game victory over Missouri, Nutt still can't believe how Jones scored what officially was a one-yard touchdown but seemed to cover more real estate than Century 21 could sell.

"That one play on the goal line," Nutt said, "he's the only one in the world who could make that play. We call a naked bootleg and they are waiting on it. He has to go back to the 10-yard line, and he is the only one who can escape a tackler, a big defensive end, and then [pull off] an unbelievable move by getting skinny sideways at the four against a corner to get in the end zone."

I Get No Respect

Even Rodney Dangerfield may have given himself more respect than Dan Doughty gives himself. Going into his fifth-year senior season of 2003, the walk-on from Clinton who earned a scholarship was among the nominees for the Rimington Award, the award annually recognizing college football's best center.

"I've been nominated for the Rimington?" Doughty asked. "Does every center get nominated?"

After Arkansas's epic, 38-28 triumph in 2003 over fifth-ranked Texas in Austin, Doughty bragged, "I know I'm the fifth-best starter on the offensive line ... and we start five."

Needless to say, Doughty didn't win the Remington. But he started every game at center for a 9-4 team that beat Missouri in the Independence Bowl, led the SEC in rushing and had senior tailback Cedric Cobbs leading the SEC in individual rushing.

Claiming His Territory

De'Arrius Howard planted an Arkansas flag on Texas turf and a target on himself. The jubilant Arkansas running back from West Memphis planted the flag outside the Razorback lockerroom in Austin after Arkansas's epic, 38-28 upset of the sixth-ranked Longhorns in 2003.

"I think I just put a bull's-eye on myself," Howard said. "We play them again next year."

If the Longhorns had anything to say about Howard after the week after the September 13 game, no media heard it. Arkansas shocked the Longhorns speechless. They didn't talk to the press all week.

The Longhorns were stewing because even their own fans were outraged. They had reacted caustically to Longhorn quotes like UT quarterback Chance Mock's summation of Arkansas's performance: "If anything, they snuck out with a win."

Proud That He's an Eagle

New Mexico State's Jimmy Cottrell might have been the first to congratulate the Philadelphia Eagles for selecting Razorback 2003 junior All-America offensive tackle Shawn Andrews in the first round of the 2004 NFL draft. New Mexico State opens Arkansas's 2004 season on September 4 in Fayetteville. And during Arkansas's 48-20 victory in 2003, Cottrell had already had seen more than enough of Andrews, particularly when the Razorbacks, like the Chicago Bears used to do with behemoth lineman Refrigerator Perry, ran the nearly 400-pound Andrews at tailback for a crushing one-yard touchdown on goal line.

"I was the first one to hit him," Cottrell said. "And that was the worst stinger in my life. I never wanna go against him again."

Some of Andrews's old offensive linemen teammates will miss him blocking on the line but might not miss the "Hurricane" surging out of the backfield as a blocking back or ballcarrier.

"The only one who didn't like it was (Razorback lineman) Zac Tubbs," Arkansas coach Houston Nutt said after Andrews debuted as a blocking back. "Because he's getting rammed in the back. But it creates a surge that's unbelievable. The guy is so athletic. He's taking care of two guys, one down lineman and one linebacker. All the backs are wanting to run in that set."

The Naked Truth

UA student Brandon Poole streaked into Razorback history by preceding Fred Talley's 63-yard streak with one against Ole Miss before a bemused Reynolds Razorback Stadium crowd at the 2002 homecoming game. Clad in nothing but a Hog hat and a G-string adorned with Colonel Reb in cover command of his privates, Poole streaked onto the field and into the Razorback huddle and out again, withstanding a shove from Arkansas left offensive tackle Bo Lacy before he was tackled by a state trooper.

The streaker was led off in handcuffs plus UA Chancellor John White's raincoat covering his bare essentials.

"I'll tell you what," Arkansas coach Houston Nutt said the following day, "the Chancellor is a team player."

The next play after the streak, Talley streaked his 63 yards, keying a 48-28 victory and starting a personal three-game streak of 241, 182 and 136 yards.

"I guess he saw the movie *Jackass* last night," Talley said, "but it really did give the offense a little time to talk. I was kind of laughing, but I guess it was a distraction to Ole Miss."

Most, but not all, of the Razorbacks were in total shock. Matt Jones, Arkansas's always laid-back quarterback, laconically confessed, "I know him. He told me this summer he was going to streak across the field. I didn't believe him, but sure enough, he was out there."

About ready to signal in a play, Nutt said he was too befuddled to laugh at the streaker's initial entry.

"I didn't know if it was part of what somebody was supposed to do for homecoming..." Nutt said, "but I saw the backside there, and I knew it wasn't part of the deal."

Mixed in with a 20-point SEC victory, the streaking incident gave a humorous respite to a team already reeling from a 29-17 loss at home the previous week to Kentucky, then shocked by the arrest of senior team captain Jermaine Brooks on felony drugs charges for which he later served time in prison.

Houston Nutt leads the charge onto the field.

"Nathan Ball (Arkansas's senior offensive guard) said it best," Nutt said the Sunday after the game. "That's really the first time we laughed all week."

Bo Lacy eventually laughed, too, though he admitted being pretty miffed at the time.

"I look up," Lacy recalled, "and there's some guy in a G-string standing right beside me. I pushed him and told him to get out of there. Then he came back again and someone said he slapped Matt on the butt and then they tackled him. I saw him out that night and he came up to me. He knew I was the guy that pushed him and he apologized to me. I said, 'No big deal, man.' He told me he was just trying to make some money out of it."

Poole got his 15 minutes of fame and set a trend.

The whole Razorback team started streaking—fully clothed, of course. The victory over Ole Miss launched a six-game win streak that carried Arkansas to the SEC West championship.

Part Two

Basketball

Don't Eat, Don't Sleep

Justin Daniel, one of Fayetteville High's better all-round athletes in the 1960s who signed a pro baseball contract after playing Razorback basketball, recalled some basketball pep talks by coach Glen Rose. Called "Gloomy Glen," Rose was almost as well-known for being taciturn as he was for being All-America both in football and basketball as a Razorback and for being the Razorbacks' winningest basketball coach until Nolan Richardson surpassed him.

"Before a game would start," Daniel recalled, "Coach Rose would say, 'Now, boys. You're not very tall. You're not very big. You are going to have to out-quick them. But the main thing is, you can't get any better by eating or sleeping.'"

Best Justin could figure, it meant don't overeat and don't sleep too much, but work out instead.

"That was his little speech," Daniel said, "that he had a few times a year. Other guys that were on the team after I was said, 'He's still making that speech. You can't get any better eating and sleeping.' He was a dandy."

A Standing O for the Big O

Tommy Rankin confessed that he was one of many Razorbacks who combined to "hold" Oscar Robertson to 56 points. An eventual NBA and collegiate Hall of Famer, Robertson scored 56 against Arkansas to pace the University of Cincinnati to a 96-62 victory over Glenn Rose's 1958 Southwest Conference Championship Razorbacks in the consolation game of the NCAA Midwest Regional.

"Oscar showed us everything in the world that night," Tommy said. "He was that good. It was just a great display of talent. Nobody could stop him. He was just awesome. He left [the game] with two minutes to go and 56 points. Twenty-thousand people gave him a standing ovation, and I was one of them. He did everything. He could have scored 66 instead of 56. I was the third one to get on him, picking him up at midcourt, and I was talking to him. He looked down at me from the top of the circle and hit the bottom of the bucket. Finally, one of our players told me to quit telling him to shoot because that wasn't helping at all. We went into a zone and still couldn't stop him. But that year we were ranked like 12th or 14th in the nation. So for an Arkansas team not supposed to do anything, it was a great year. We weren't supposed to win, but we've got our banner down at Walton Arena right now."

Rebel Without a Pause

Rankin was quite the outside shooter in his Jonesboro High School days and was recruited hotly by the Ole Miss Rebels. He was influenced on his Ole Miss visit to sign with Arkansas by a Rebel without a pause.

"Country Graham was the Ole Miss basketball coach," Rankin said, "Country knew he was fighting Arkansas recruiting me, with it being the first year of Barnhill Fieldhouse. He looked out the gym door of Ole Miss and said, 'I know Arkansas has a new gym. Son, we're building a new gym here at Ole Miss and you can play in that.' I told one of the Ole Miss players about the new gym. He was reading a magazine and didn't even look up. 'That's the same crap he told me two years ago,' he said."

So Tommy signed the standard no-frills agreement with Rose. Arkansas's taciturn coach always offered the same deal no matter what other school was in the running for that player.

"You talk about Coach Rose," Tommy said, "you are talking about a piece of art. He'd reach that right hand over to

Coach "Gloomy Glen" Rose—a real piece of work.

scratch his left ear and talk to you. Coach Rose said, 'You've got a bus ticket to come up here and a scholarship to go to school on. I'm not buying a big man, and I'm not buying a little man. If I've got to buy one, I've got to buy another.'"

Gloomy Glen Shows a Heart

After watching Tommy Rankin injure his back, Glen Rose went forward with compassion.

"We were playing Ole Miss," Tommy recalled, "and a ball started rolling out of bounds. I bent down to get it and couldn't, went after it again and still couldn't reach it and it rolled out of bounds with me looking directly into Coach Rose's eyes. Coach Rose pulled me aside and said, 'I'm putting you on the bench. You are going to be my sixth man again these next two years. If I need you, I need you. Just make your grades and graduate. My back is worn out from playing football and basketball, and I know what it's like. I don't want this to happen to you.' It was a hard pill for me to swallow at the time. I almost left over it because I thought I could play, but I respect him for it now. That's experience and maturity showing. Coach Rose was a fine man."

No Reunions

Ricky Tanneberger advised Razorback seniors on the struggling 2002-2003 team to remember each other well. Chances are, they won't much see their teammates through the years. Tanneberger knows because he was a senior on Duddy Waller's final Razorback team that went 5-19 in 1970.

"I read a book by Pat Conroy called *My Losing Season*," Tanneberger said. "He was at The Citadel in 1966. They were picked to do well and didn't. This book goes game by game with the few they won and the more they lost. He said something at the beginning of the book that is true. 'If you are on a winning team, then you have reunions and people come back and live the glory days and the wives know each other ...and all that. If you are on a losing team, you go out with no fanfare and probably never associate.' You don't come back to celebrate a 5-19 season and have Razorback reunions to celebrate your senior year. We never did.

"But look at the '64 (national championship) football team, they seem to have [reunions] all the time."

Close but No Cigar

Like the players from this last Razorback team, Tanneberger can recall many "close but no cigar" games during his senior year.

"We had some games we played well," Tanneberger said, "but we couldn't get over the hump. A lot like [the 2003] team. A lot of similarities. We lost about seven by three points or less. Win those and we're 12-12 instead of 5-19, and Duddy wouldn't have been fired. I remember him telling us with about three or four games to go he wouldn't be back."

Sometimes just plain bad luck can make a mediocre team go bad.

"My senior year we played Mississippi State in the Liberty Bowl Classic," Tanneberger said. "This was before the clock showed tenths of seconds. The ball was out of bounds at half-court, and the clock showed zero and the score was tied. They passed the ball to a guy at the top of the circle. He turned around and jumped up and shot the ball, not in one motion, with the clock showing zero, but they counted it. The officials went over to the scorer's table and the official scorer said the horn hadn't sounded. So we lost after they inbounded and made a shot with no time on the clock. We played SMU at Dallas and were ahead by one. They had the ball out of bounds with two seconds left under their basket. Gene Phillips, their All-Southwest Conference player, caught the ball on the inbounds pass in the corner, fell out of bounds and threw it up there. It wasn't a shot—he just threw it up there. It hit on top of the backboard, and bounced up and rolled down through it. We lost at Texas Tech on a last-second shot, and lost at TCU the last game of the season by two."

Proof for the Flat Earth Society

Had Christopher Columbus seen some of the basketballs that Duddy Waller's Razorbacks had to practice with, America might still be undiscovered.

"The program was a lot different," Tanneberger said. "They had some good (basketball) teams in the '50s, but football was the sport, and we were a secondary deal. I'd never trade it in a million years and I loved the experience and the team and everything else, but we played at Barnhill when they used the court for Fourth Quarter (off season) football. They might have mopped the court, and they might not. There would be a sawdust film on it when you came to practice. And we always came to practice early. Because the balls that you practiced with, if you came early, you'd go find a ball that was round. If you got there late, some of them were lopsided. They had a basket of 20 of them and about 75 percent might [be lopsided]... That was kind of the way we had it."

Duddy Did Integrate UA Hoops

Though winning wasn't a constant, some landmark developments did occur during the Waller era.

Arkansas integrated its basketball team.

Almer Lee and Vernon Murphy often get recalled as the Razorbacks' first black basketball players, but that wasn't the case, Tanneberger said.

"Thomas Johnson from Menifee was," Tanneberger said. "T.J. played freshman ball all year, then transferred to UCA. By the time I was a senior then Almer (from Fort Smith) had come up from Phillips Junior College in Helena and Vernon Murphy from Texarkana had been recruited. T.J., you couldn't have found a better guy to recruit as the first."

Unlike some of his UA teammates, Tanneberger already had played on an integrated team at Little Rock Central High.

"Central had integrated and had its first black basketball player, Kenneth Robinson," Tanneberger said. "The strange thing about it—Kenneth Robinson's brother is David Robinson's (of NBA fame) dad. I didn't know that until about 10 years ago when there was an article about it."

Tanneberger said Arkansas's basketball integration "went very smoothly. There was never any problem in the transition from an all-white team to an integrated one."

Only Waller busted a gut—and that was inadvertent. For a previously all-white program, Almer Lee was an enigma—not because of color, but style.

"Almer, with his behind-the-back passing and behind-the-back dribbling was kind of a new deal," Tanneberger said. "And he shot the ball from outside. If he was having a good game, he played a lot. If he wasn't hitting his shot, he didn't play. Because with Duddy, if you didn't pass it 10 times before you shot it, then you'd better make the shot."

Here's what Duddy apparently couldn't stomach.

"The night before the big Arkansas-Texas football shootout in '69," Tanneberger said, "we played [coach] Hank Iba and Oklahoma State at our place. It was Almer's first game. Iba had a lead and was running the stall, and we finally steal the ball down five points, and Almer broke and we got the ball to him—uncontested layup. He takes the ball at the free throw line dribbling and puts it behind the back and shoots the layup, and the referee calls walking on him. Almer hadn't walked. But the referee had never seen anyone put it behind his back before. [The ref] disallows the basket and we never caught up and lost by five. And this was Duddy coaching against Hank Iba and he was really, really hot. He said, 'I'm going to let you all go to the football game, but we will practice Sunday afternoon!' He made it evident that not too many people would be able to walk after that Sunday practice. We go to practice and the trainer says, 'Did you hear about Duddy?' He had an appendicitis attack and got rushed to the hospital!"

Lights Out

Almer Lee, the Razorbacks' first black scholarship basketball player, recalled how he shot lights out and impressed the younger Ron Brewer Sr. Brewer idolized Lee as both grew up in Fort Smith.

"We go back [to] the projects," Lee said. "Ron as a little boy would come out to the park when I was working out by myself at night. He would retrieve the ball and pass the ball back to me and watch the moves I was trying to develop. As a little boy he said, 'Wow—how can you do that? And how can you hit those shots in the dark?' I'd say, 'If I can make those in the dark, imagine what I can do when it's light.'"

However, Lee, a Razorback under Duddy Waller in 1970 and Lanny Van Eman in 1971, said it was Brewer who really was the shining light as one of Eddie Sutton's fabled Triplets with the Razorbacks from 1976-78. Lee also foresees Ronnie Brewer, Ron's son and a starting freshman guard for Stan Heath's Razorbacks in 2003-2004, doing the same as his father.

"When I see Ronnie," Lee said. "I see a replica of his dad. And his dad to me is the best player ever to play up here. There wasn't anything he couldn't do."

Pain in the Glass

L anny Van Eman sometimes seemed more fast-talking used-car dealer than head basketball coach. But the predecessor to Eddie Sutton did guide Arkansas into modern basketball by recruiting such talented black players as Martin Terry and Dean Tolson. Two years before Van Eman gave way to Sutton, his 1972-73 team went 16-10, the first Razorback winning season since Glenn Rose's 1965-66 Hogs went 13-10. The '72-73 bunch tied for second in the SWC and were in the championship hunt until losing a 64-63 heartbreaker at a packed Barnhill Fieldhouse to Texas Tech in the season's second to last game.

The next day, Lanny recalled, he received a call from athletic director George Cole. Basketball hadn't hit the UA's big-time support yet. Maybe this would be a turning point.

"I come into his office," Van Eman said, "expecting him to say something like, 'Good job. That was a tough one and you almost won it.' Instead he grumbled, 'Van Eman, some fan broke the glass out of one of the doors carrying on after the basketball game. We can't have that.'"

A Paneful Entrance

B efore the Broyles Complex was built, all the Razorback coaches and staff had their offices in Barnhill Fieldhouse: Greg Mills, a student assistant in the sports information department during the '70s, was working late one night on the second floor when he heard a rustling by the window. It was more than a rustling. In through the window climbed basketball player Jack Schulte followed by his date.

"Shhh!" Schulte told the startled Mills. "I always do this when they are having a concert. Beats paying for tickets."

There was a rock concert in Barnhill that night, and Jack and his date presumably got in free.

Playing two years for Lanny Van Eman and two years for Eddie Sutton, Schulte was a big man (6-8, 220) who could shoot outside and once even outplayed Robert Parish, the Centenary great who became the "Chief" as the Boston Celtics' longtime center. Schulte's sizable talent was only exceeded by his lack of attention span. Jack jacked shots at the most inopportune times, like in the middle of Sutton's "five-game", which was a variation of Dean Smith's four-corners when only a layup was permitted.

"No, Jack, no!" Sutton would scream as Schulte squared up.

Ashen, Sutton would sigh, "Good, Jack, good," as it swished home.

"Jack Schulte's elevator didn't go all the way to the top," former Arkansas teammate Steve Price mused. "Jack would stand right under the basket and jump up and try and block shots. He couldn't figure out that if you stood right under the basket and blocked shots it was going to be called goaltending. He would try and block 15-foot shots standing under the basket, and Coach Sutton would stop practice and holler, 'Jack, you can't do that!' Schulte got hollered at more than anybody, without a doubt. But he was so strong and he could shoot—he was a heck of a talent. If they had the three-point line then, he could shoot it out there."

Nailing His Shot

Jack sometimes literally nailed his shot, recalled Jimmy Counce, fabled as the defensive forward during the Triplets era, but just a freshman and sophomore pup when Schulte played.

"Jack was a great shooter for a guy his size," Counce recalled. "But he had got his thumb caught in a teeter totter when he was young and had no nail bed, just a little nail kind of growing out of his thumb. Every once in a while he'd get where he couldn't hit a shot. He'd look at that thumb and think the nail was too long, and he'd go rub it on a concrete block, kind of like a bear scratching a post. He'd do that and his shooting touch would be back, and he'd just shrug. Jack was one of the most unique people I ever met."

Tape Shredder

About the time one of president Richard Nixon's Watergate tapes was discovered to have an 18-minute gap, one of Jimmy Counce's tapes was gapped entirely.

Jack Schulte was the shredder.

"Jack had a '68 Impala," Counce said, "and asked me if he could borrow an Elton John eight-track tape to take along while he was having a date. His tape player ate my tape alive. He walks in and says, 'Here's your tape.' The cartridge is completely torn apart and there's this huge wad of tape. I ask, 'What happened?'

"And he says, 'I don't know. I guess something is wrong with it.'"

Way Out West

Jack was from Ellisville, Missouri, and went to Subiaco Academy before eventually moving out to California. The last time I saw Jack breeze back through Fayetteville, I asked what he was doing.

"I'm just a 25-year-old jerk that's out of work," Schulte said.

A space cadet—maybe—but never a jerk.

"Jack Schulte," teammate Marvin Delph said. "That was one guy that would do anything for you."

Almer Recruits a Triplet

Former Arkansas coach Eddie Sutton and former Arkansas assistant coach Pat Foster are credited with recruiting Razorback Hall of Honor member Ron (Boot) Brewer out of Fort Smith Northside. But, according to Brewer, another man recruited him more than those two coaches.

If Almer Lee hadn't voted thumbs up on the Hogs, Arkansas would have had twins—Conway's Marvin Delph and Sidney Moncrief of Little Rock Hall—instead of the fabled Triplets of Brewer. Lee was the Northside star Brewer looked up to as Almer went on to play at the UA for Duddy Waller. Then, in Brewer's view, Lee's role got shortchanged in the switch from Waller to Lanny Van Eman, Sutton's immediate successor.

"Martin Terry was his superstar," Brewer said of Van Eman. "Martin could score, but I didn't like the way it was handled. I didn't think they had treated Almer fairly. And because of that I didn't want to come up here. Coach Sutton knew that and he told Almer, 'Tell Ron those days are over with.' Almer gave me a foundation. If you asked me, who turned my game around? It was Almer Lee. He showed me so much. He's the one."

Not Just the Triplets

The death of Steve Stroud at 48 to pancreatic cancer in January of 2003 underscored to Brewer his often expressed sentiments that the Razorbacks of his time were a lot more than just the Triplets.

"The Triplets were marketed well," Brewer said. "But people don't understand the significance of Steve Stroud, Jimmy Counce and Steve Schall and the defense they played."

Stroud was especially known for his post defense and Schall for his offense as the alternating center tandem on the 1976-77 Hogs that went unbeaten in the Southwest Conference and 26-2 for the season.

"Steve Stroud was a big, integral part of our success," Brewer said. "He was our enforcer, closing down the middle, blocking shots, playing defense, and he scored in there as well. Most of all he was a great friend. He will be deeply missed."

Talking about the extremely physical, 6-10, 240-pound fifth-year senior, Stroud brought to mind the bloodletting that passed for practice in the Sutton era.

"Practice in general was a war for all Razorbacks," Brewer said. "A lot of stitches, swollen eyes, bloody noses, some concussions and knocked-out teeth. If you could survive practice, games were fun."

Big Blue Hog Callers

Aside from his buzzer-beater to edge Notre Dame in the consolation game, Brewer's best memories of the 1978 Final Four in St. Louis came from Kentucky fans.

"It was fantastic," Brewer said of playing in the Final Four. "The aura of enthusiastic fans. You are talking Kentucky, Notre Dame, Arkansas and Duke. You couldn't ask for a better group of fans. When we got beat by Kentucky, their people started getting on board and called the Hogs during the consolation game. That was really nice."

Legitimizing the Program

Though Arkansas went 26-2 in 1976-77, the first-round NCAA Tournament loss to Wake Forest had the national media skeptical until the '78 Hogs beat UCLA, 74-70 in the second round of the NCAA Tournament.

Beating UCLA, even if it was post-John Wooden, seemed to be the game that nationally legitimized the Hogs.

"It was and it wasn't," Brewer said. "I know more than anybody they weren't the UCLA of old. But I do know this— there was a tradition, an aura there. Just by beating UCLA, it was a breakthrough."

What If?

Although the Triplets excelled in Sutton's system, what if the 6-4 trio played for a coach whose system didn't count passes like insomniacs count sheep? How many points might they have averaged?

"I thought about that after I came back to the University of Arkansas," Brewer said, "and saw Coach Richardson's system. First thing I thought of is it would be nice to see how many points I could have averaged because we didn't have that type of freedom. Any player would love to be a part of that, because it's a player's game. But you've got to have the players to play that."

Nolan Richardson was coaching the Razorbacks when Brewer, after a long career in the NBA, came back to the UA to earn his degree. Now he watches his son Ronnie, a prep standout from Fayetteville who immediately stood out as a freshman starting guard for Stan Heath's Razorbacks in 2003-2004. Ronnie Brewer turned down offers from programs doing well, like Oklahoma and the Eddie Sutton-coached Oklahoma State Cowboys, to stay home even though the Hogs had suffered two

Ron Brewer Sr. was one-third of Eddie Sutton's fabled Triplets. Today, he enjoys watching his son play for coach Stan Heath.

straight losing seasons, 14-15 under Richardson and 9-19 under Heath.

"I told him, 'Ronnie, I lost more games my first year at Arkansas than I had my whole career from junior high through high school,'" Brewer said. "But the next year we went 26-2. They had to get players in place like the University of Arkansas is trying to do now. You've got to project yourself in the picture and what you can do to help your team. You do that, it doesn't matter where you go. Because the system is going to be the same, the academic setup is going to be pretty much the same. If you can play, you can play."

Ronnie Brewer showed he can play. While Arkansas's improvement was still gradual, 12-16 for 2003-2004, Brewer so excelled that he was named to the All-SEC Freshman team and was runnerup in SEC Freshman of the Year voting.

Listen to the Doctor Operate

Dr. Jim Counce can operate as a storyteller as readily as he operates on hearts. Known as Jimmy Counce when he was the role-playing, seldom-scoring, defensive ace forward for Eddie Sutton's 1977 and '78 teams that went 26-2 and 32-4, the cardiologist's best tales don't involve the Triplets.

"We weren't all that good, but things were more amusing then," Counce said of Sutton's first two teams when Jimmy was a freshman and sophomore in 1974-75 and '75-76 before the Triplets became stars.

Previous coach Lanny Van Eman left some characters and some players, and some who were both, such as junior guard Robert Birden of Pine Bluff.

In Eddie's first televised Southwest Conference game against SMU, Birden's outside shooting rang through SMU's triangle and two defense during a second-half surge that won a 73-69 thriller in Dallas. The Raycom TV crew doing the game pounced on Birden for the postgame interview, apparently oblivious that a gravel-voiced Lithuanian with a sock in his mouth was easier to understand than "Birdman," as Birden called himself.

"They interview Birden after the game," Counce recalled, and ask him, 'Robert what was it that got into you that second half?'

"Robert strokes his goatee and says, 'Uh, well, you know, man, when you're hot, you're hot.'"

Drafting a Nickname

"Birdman had a nickname for everybody," Counce said. "Jack Schulte was 'Wolfman.' Birden called Dan Pauley, 'Keghead.' He said the reason he called Dan Keghead is because his head was as big as a keg."

Phantom Jet

Lanny Van Eman's best gift to the Sutton regime actually came after Lanny was first gone from the Hogs and had become an assistant at Western Kentucky. Western Kentucky had a 6-7 Ohio Valley Conference forward, Kent Allison, who had been declared ineligible to play his senior year at WKU but could transfer with immediate eligibility anywhere else, much like Razorback Sunday Adebayo had to do by NCAA decree in 1997. Lanny called Pat Foster, his top UA assistant retained by Sutton, and relayed that Allison was now a recruitable athlete.

"Kent had scheduled a visit to come here," Counce said. "But in the meantime he visited somewhere else and decided that's where he wanted to go. He called Coach Sutton and said, 'Listen, I'm not going to come because I've already decided.'

And Coach Sutton says, 'Wait! You can't do that! We've already got a plane in the air to come get you.' So Kent says, 'Okay.' Coach Sutton hangs up, makes another call and says, 'Get that plane up in the air!'"

Without that deception, Sutton's inaugural season might well have been 9-17 instead of 17-9. Allison's inside play carried those Hogs.

"What a difference Kent made," Counce said. "If not for a horrible call at Texas A&M, we would have won the conference. Darryl Saulsberry has a breakaway and lays the ball in, because there was a no-dunk rule. It was a layup, not a dunk, but they void the basket."

Arkansas lost, 62-60.

Madhatters

If anybody deserved to beat Arkansas on a bad call that year, it probably was A&M coach Shelby Metcalf. Shelby and his Aggies really had a rough time of it in 1975 at Barnhill Fieldhouse. Not only did they lose, 85-79 in double overtime, but they were harrassed by the "Madhatters," a group of Razorback football players led by offensive lineman Greg Koch and recruited by Sutton to sit behind the Aggie bench. The players arrived in wild costumes and constantly heckled the Aggies.

"Shelby was trying to huddle with his players," Counce said, "and he looked up one time, and there was Greg Koch with his head stuck in the huddle with that gorilla mask on."

By the third timeout, the Aggies were huddling at mid-court, lugging their chairs behind them.

Seems the Aggies were a chair short after the first two timeouts because the Madhatters would nab one after they were vacated while the team huddled around Metcalf.

"You couldn't get away with that stuff now," Counce said.

Deep in the Heart O' Texas

Those 1975 basketball Razorbacks could have survived the loss at A&M if they just could have beaten a bad Baylor team at Heart O' Texas Coliseum in Waco. Baylor's dimly lit rodeo ground of a basketball coliseum never was a Sutton favorite.

"You'd always think some cowboy was going to come out and rope a steer," Sutton would say.

Sutton hated playing there. He wasn't alone.

"Everybody hated it," Counce said. "It was so depressing to play there. Waco was depressing. The crowd was depressing. The floor was set on concrete. And we'd lose to not very good Baylor teams. That was really depressing."

Even the 32-4 Final Four team in 1978 barely escaped defeat, 56-55, in overtime at Heart 'O Texas.

The Goose at DFW

While Sutton inherited a few characters, he brought in some doozies, too. Two in particular that Counce recalled who caused Sutton and assistants Pat Foster and Gene Keady a few gray hairs were roommates Ken "Goose" Gehring and Corky Corzine.

Until Nolan Richardson's 1994 Razorbacks, Gehring may have been the only Razorback to play on a national championship basketball team. He had been a backup for North Carolina State's national champions before transferring to Arkansas for the 1977-78 season.

"He and Corky bought some junk car for $25," Counce said, "and had all the parts laid out in their room."

For awhile, it appeared DFW Airport security was going to have Gehring permanently in one room.

"They had huge signs," Counce said, "at every security entrance saying 'Bombs and weapons are no laughing matter. We take every statement seriously. Do not joke about bombs or weapons.' So of course Goose Gehring says at the DFW Airport right in front of the security, 'Hey, Corky! What did you do with that bomb you had in your bag?' They immediately hauled him off and the Feds are interrogating him. I think it took quite a bit of persuasion from Coach Sutton and Coach Keady to get him released. But not [until] after they scared him quite a bit. And you didn't want to be released to Coach Keady's custody. I think you would have been much better off with the Feds. I believe I would have said, 'I would rather stay.'"

That's the same Gene Keady whose face resembles a clenched fist on TV as he coaches Purdue.

Love in Brazil

A Razorback freshman in 1976-77, Lawson Pilgrim transferred back to his hometown and Hendrix College in Conway in '77-78, but not before almost transferring to Brazil. The 1976 26-2 squad got an NCAA-sanctioned postseason trip to Brazil to play several games there.

"He met some girl in Brazil," Counce said. "She didn't speak any English, and he didn't speak any Portugese, but they were cooing and gooing. We got ready to leave on a Sunday. We had played pretty well, but we were tired and sick of the food and had played this exhibition game and just got waxed. The bus picks us up and nobody can find Lawson. Nobody knows where he is."

Some wanted to look more than others.

"Coach Sutton says, 'It's time to go. We've got to go to the airport. We're leaving him,'" Counce recalled. "We're thinking, 'Lawson is in a foreign country in a city of eight million. He'll never get back! We can't leave him!' But sure enough, we pull out from the arena and we're on Ipanema Boulevard. We're thinking Lawson is stuck in Brazil. We came to a traffic light a long way from the arena, and we look out and there is this bench at a bus stop, and there's Lawson with this girl saying good-bye. They both have tears in their eyes and we yell, 'Lawson! Get on the bus!' We open the door and Lawson gets on. And I have no idea how he got there or how we could somehow drive right by [him]."

No Rand McNally

Graduating from Hendrix, Lawson Pilgrim obviously has some major brainpower going for him, but he did suffer a geography lapse, Counce remembered. It was during a stretch when they had postseason practices to prepare for Brazil.

"I remember we're in Wilson Sharp tossing a medicine ball back and forth," Counce said. "And Lawson says, 'Jim, I wonder what it's like in Europe.'

"And I said, 'I don't know, Lawson. I've never been.'

"And he says, 'Well, I guess we'll find out when we get to Brazil.'"

Lawson had method to his malaprops in his reference to fellow freshman Alan Zahn's hometown, Albuquerque, N.M.

"Alan was always on Lawson," Counce said "and Lawson would say, 'Oh, Zahn. Why don't you go back to Albuturkey?'"

Wrong Comrade

After Wake Forest used a press to come back from a huge deficit and beat the 26-2 1977 Razorbacks in the first round of the NCAA Tournament, Sutton sought press-breaking help in junior college transfer point guard Mike Buckrop. Buckrop wasn't the answer. He only lasted a semester.

"'Buck,' as we called him," Counce said laughing. "We played the Russian National team in Little Rock. We were up in the training room talking about the Russians, and Alan Zahn said, 'I wonder if we could return the game next year and go to Moscow and play?' And Buck gave this disgusted snort and said, 'Are you crazy, man? Castro would never allow it.'"

Fidel, the Aussie?

Now Counce wouldn't have been surprised to learn Castro had been involved with the Australian government, considering some of the wild Australian tennis players the Hogs had during that 1970s era. The boys from Down Under were over the top hecklers at basketball and baseball games in the 1970s.

"You remember when Castro opened up the prisons and sent them [to the United States]?" Counce said. "I think Australia did the same thing with tennis players."

Not a Cheap Shot

Counce probably could have sold a few books and gone on talk shows saying he suffered a life-threatening injury because of Bill Laimbeer, one of the alleged cheap-shot Detroit Pistons "Bad Boys." A collision with Laimbeer during the 1978 Hogs' Final Four consolation game victory over Notre Dame meant Counce had to part with some of his kidney on an operating table in St. Louis.

"I can't blame that on him," Counce said. "It was a two-on-one break and I ran over him and he kind of flopped, and then I fell down on top of him. He had his elbow braced to pro-

tect his head, and I came down right on top of him. I got up and
ran down the floor and suddenly I thought I was going to
puke—just an incredible wave of nausea. Coach got me out and
(trainer) Mike McDonald took me back to the locker room. I
didn't hurt at all, and I had a couple of dry heaves and my nausea went away. I thought I would go back in, but the NCAA had
physicians on the bench and this doctor said, 'Before you go
back out there, let me press around on your belly a little bit.' He
touched that spot where I got hit, and I almost shot out of uniform it hurt so bad. He said, 'You aren't going anywhere but to
the hospital.' I don't remember much after that. It was a rup-
tured kidney and they were operating.

"I stayed in that St. Louis hospital from Monday night
until Sunday, and then was in the hospital here in Fayetteville
three or four more days. My teammates were very supportive.
Back at the dorm they divvied [up] my stuff. Steve Schall had
my car keys."

What a Time to Resign

Counce had a 100-percent solid excuse for not finishing the
Razorbacks' final game at the 1978 Final Four in St. Louis.
But another player, Michael Watley, inexplicably chose not to go
to St. Louis.

"The only guy I know," Counce said, "who quit after winning the West Regional as we're about to go to the Final Four.
He was mad because he wasn't playing. He was behind Ron
Brewer, Marvin Delph and Sidney Moncrief and didn't think he
was getting enough time.

"He thought he was better than what he was—obviously."

Put My Fake Teeth in Your Crooked Eye

As a freshman in 1974-75, Counce's mouth was discovered by teammate Daryll Saulserry's elbow during practice. The result of the blow was missing teeth, with Counce eventually playing with a plastic plate he'd put loosely in his mouth to take their place.

Counce's fake teeth, and his shooting, two rarities figuring in any story, figured prominently in this one. It involved the 1976-77 Hogs eking by Southwest Missouri State, 72-71 in Springfield, Missouri for the second game of the season.

"They were opening the Hammons Center," Counce said, "and asked if we would open it in the inaugural game. We didn't know whether we were any good, and they had a little left-handed guard who hit 42 [points] on us. We're hanging on by the skin of our teeth, and their crowd is going bananas. They missed a shot that would have won the game with about five or six seconds to go when we had a one-point lead. Their guard shot and missed, and I got the rebound and got fouled. It was a one and one. I missed the free throw, they got the rebound and threw up a halfcourt shot that missed, and we ran off the floor thinking we had won."

Officials didn't think along the same line.

"We were in the locker room," Counce said, "most of us getting in the shower, when the officials came in. They said we would have to replay the final five or six seconds because Southwest Missouri State had only four legal players on the floor because the guy that fouled me had fouled out of the game and they hadn't allowed them the chance to substitute. The officials said it was their fault, a correctable error, and the game should resume. Coach Sutton said he would not go out and replay it. We were showering, going home and taking the W," Counce continued.

"The officials said," Counce related, 'If you don't go back out, [Arkansas will] forfeit the game to Southwest Missouri State.' Coach Sutton said, 'We'll replay from where we shot the

Jimmy Counce—now Dr. Jim Counce—grabs a rebound. Counce tells Hogs stories with as much ease as he operates on hearts.

free throws.' So we go out there thinking we're getting jobbed in a home-cooking type of deal. And I'm thinking the scorekeeper is involved.

"Now this is 20 minutes after the game had supposedly ended, and we go back out and the whole crowd is still there. They didn't give us a chance to warm up or anything. We line up again and this time, fortunately, I hit the free throws, and there is no three-point shot at the time."

Thus, despite an uncontested SMS field goal after Counce's free throws, the Bears were still a point short.

"So I go up to the scorekeeper," Counce said, "and say, 'That's in your crooked eye.' Well, unfortunately when I did that, my plate fell completely out of my mouth and I caught it just before it tumbled out on the floor. Poor guy. He looked at me like I was crazy. I thought this was kind of embarrassing. I didn't know what else to do but pop it back in my mouth and walk off."

Rerouting Walker's Walkout

Darrell Walker had to have been the only Razorback basketball player to quit the team and be the only player watching game film as the rest partied. Calling from Italy where he was scouting international prospects for the Washington Wizards, Walker laughed, recalling that bizarre turnaround.

Eddie Sutton's Razorbacks had just won one of their most thrilling games ever at Barnhill Arena on a Scott Hastings buzzer beater over the Houston Cougars featuring Hakeem Olajuwon and Clyde Drexler. Hastings's shot just made it over the outstretched hand of Olajuwon, who came out of nowhere.

Walker celebrated by storming off the court vowing to quit the team. Darrell's anger had nothing to do with not wanting the Hogs to win, but with not being a part of it when it counted.

"It was a fast break," Walker recalled. "Coach Sutton pulled me out because I didn't give it up and pass off on a break. I got mad. Right after the game I put my sweatsuit on and walked out."

It was presumed Walker had quit the team. But finishing his game story late, an exiting reporter chanced on Walker. Darrell had still been in Barnhill happily watching game film. Somebody stopped Walker's walk from becoming Walker's walk-out.

"It was U.S. Reed's mother," Walker said, citing the mother of one of his teammates. "She talked me into calming down and I did."

Lemons Sweetens Bitter Past

Walker's biggest brouhaha on the basketball court came during a melee with Texas, coached by the witty but irascible Abe Lemons. In those Southwest Conference days, with Arkansas being the lone SWC team not based in Texas, any incident with the University of Texas was going to bring the wrath of the Lone Star state.

"Ray Harper (a Texas guard) and I had got into it at Barnhill," Walker said. "It was Ray Harper and Scott (Hastings) at first, and I got into it and whacked Harper. And Abe went to the Commissioner and said I should have been suspended."

Subsequent film indicated some Longhorns could have been subjected to disciplinary action as easily as Walker. So no action was taken.

Later that season, an incident flared in another Razorback game. Walker most definitely was not involved. When the shoving started he raced to the middle of the court and sat down. The laughter helped defuse the fracas. As the post Arkansas-Texas focus started riveting on Lemons's conduct instead of Walker, Abe's Texas tenure began unraveling.

Too bad, Walker laments sincerely.

"Abe was something else," Walker said. "I ran into Abe after he was doing TV and we had a good conversation. He said something funny. We got along great other than that one incident. Abe was a good coach. Nobody gave him credit for that because he was so funny. But Abe was also a really good coach."

Watching U.S. Reed hit the buzzer-beating halfcourt shot to beat Louisville in the NCAA Tournament after Louisville had just gone ahead on a basket scored off a steal against Arkansas's Mike Young in Austin, Lemons was reported to have advised Young, "Son, you need to thank Reed for saving your scholarship."

Abe was pretty funny as a TV color commentator. Once, to Lemons's obvious delight, Guy Lewis's Houston Cougars were beating the bejabbers out of the Texas team that had just fired Abe.

"Guy is trying to hold this score down," Lemons told the TV audience. "He's played everybody. Oh, wait, he hasn't played the Bunce brothers (the camera panned on two huge bookends on the Cougar bench). How would you like to feed those guys?"

Number, Please

No walk-on anywhere could have been any more beloved than Eugene Nash, the guard out of little Tyronza who joined Eddie Sutton's Razorbacks and by his senior year had all of Barnhill Arena chanting "Eu-Gene! Eu-Gene! Eu-Gene!" Turns out the walk-on walked a long path right over senior legend Sidney Moncrief to get his chance to make the team.

"I wrote a letter to Coach Sutton giving him a little history on my stats and [saying] that I would like to walk on," Eugene, now an executive at Tyson Foods in Springdale, recalled. "He sent a letter back welcoming me to the UA and about their program. At that time, he said he hadn't kept walk-ons but they would have tryouts. There had to be over 150 guys trying out. It whittled to 100, and then they picked six guys. We did that for two days, and then it was down to two players. The next day that guy didn't show back up. I ended up being the lone guy."

That didn't mean Eugene had made the team, however, assistant coach Bob Cleeland said.

"Coach Cleeland walked over," Eugene said, "He went through the same spiel. 'We've got enough players, it might be your last day, and if it is, Coach Sutton will come over and talk to you.' I looked in the mirror and said, 'Today could be your last day in organized basketball.' I was blocking everyone's shot. I goaltended a James Crockett (Crockett stood 6-9 and Nash, 6-1) shot. I blocked Sidney's shot. Coach Sutton said, 'Do you know you are goal tending?'

"Afterwards I was shooting free throws by myself, and lo and behold here comes a rebounder for me—Coach Sutton. I keep waiting for the axe to fall. He gathered us back up started to walk away and then said, 'By the way, what number do you want?'"

One of Their Own

Students cheered for Sidney Moncrief in Eugene's day because Sidney was the best. Then when Sidney graduated, they cheered for Scott Hastings because he was the best. But though he seldom played when the game was on the line until late in his career, students cheered loudest for Eugene, because he was one of their own.

"I think the reason that happened is not living in the athletic dorm," Nash said. "I mingled with the student body. A group from Hotz Hall said, 'We've been watching you progress. We think you should be playing. So when you're not playing, we're going to start chanting Eu-Gene, Eu-Gene!' I cracked up. And I said, 'What good is that going to do?'

"I played that night. Coach Sutton gave us a speech that night about being a Razorback, that the fans love you. 'A great example is what they are doing for Eugene,' he said. 'We've got to be role models. Don't walk away from a child who wants an autograph.'"

My Other Brother, Darrell

Eugene Nash said he took to heart Eddie Sutton's edict about signing every autograph. He still does even today as "even now I get recognized," Nash said. He's convinced, though, that the fans remembering those teams he played for think they'll get someone else's autograph when they get his.

"I think they think I'm Darrell Walker," Nash said of his far more famous old teammate. "Me and Darrell had little, bitty heads. The funny thing now is you meet people who say they got my autograph when they were five years old. I look at them now and they are bigger than me. I think if I hadn't signed them, it could be ugly for me now."

More Than a Crowd Favorite

Nearly all of Eugene's playing time had been at home with the students chanting to put him once the game was safely tucked away. That's why Eugene nearly went into shock in Austin one night.

"Down in Texas," Nash recalled, "Coach Sutton came to my room. I was rooming with Darrell (Walker) and that's who I thought he was looking for. He said, 'Well actually I'm here to see you. We've been keeping an eye on you.'

"I had beaten Mike Young, an excellent shooter, in a game of Horse in the shootaround. Coach said, 'If these guys don't do well, we may use you.'"

What a shock! Counted upon at Texas.

"So as much as you want to win," Nash said, "you think, 'If these guys mess up, it might be my chance.' U.S. (Reed) did miss his first three shots. When U.S. missed those first three shots, Coach walked down, looked at me, and I think he was thinking, 'I'm going to do this.'

"But he turned back and U.S. turned it on. But I did get in without anybody having to chant. I played early in the second half at Austin. Coach said he wanted to put me in the game earlier but he didn't want to read headlines, 'Eddie Lost His Mind.'"

Last but Not Least

Eugene's first start was his last home game. He was one of six seniors, and the best one, the one who had started every game since breaking into the lineup in the season opener as a freshman, yielded the floor to Eugene Nash on Senior Night against Baylor.

"Scott Hastings gave up his spot," Nash said. "Scott went to Coach and said, 'I know you'd like to start seniors, and while this game means a lot to me, I want Eugene to have my spot.' He was very gracious."

The "Eu-Gene! Eu-Gene! Eu-Gene!," chants ricocheted off the Barnhill walls well beyond the actual tipoff.

"That was a big night," Nash said. "That's the night that always stands out."

Legend Sidney Moncrief—leaping for a rebound—wants everyone to know that Eddie Sutton's Triplets never played slow ... just as fast as they needed to.

Not So Fast

Recalling his Razorback career from 1976-79 under Eddie Sutton, All-American Sidney Moncrief says, "The good thing is I don't have any bad memories."

Just one false impression to correct.

"It bothers me when people say we played slow," Moncrief said of the Sutton style that took Arkansas to Southwest Conference championships in three of Moncrief's four years—plus a Final Four and an Elite Eight appearance. "We just played as fast as we needed to."

Moncrief recalls winning a lot more games with Arkansas scoring in the '70s and '80s than the 41-38 and 43-35 chess matches over Texas Tech and TCU in 1977.

"Those were the teams stalling the ball," Moncrief said. "People would see those scores and say, 'There goes Arkansas slowing it down again when it was the opposing coach who was controlling the offense with a stall.'"

A Confidence Boost

For a player to get praise from Sutton and assistants Pat Foster and Gene Keady, he really had to earn it. That's why even before NBC's Al McGuire nationally dubbed them the Triplets, Moncrief, Ron Brewer and Marvin Delph nearly went into shock in the preseason before their 1977-78 team soared to the Final Four.

"Coach Sutton called us all in the office," Moncrief said, "and told us, 'You guys don't really know how good you all can be. You all are as good as any players in the country.' I think that pushed us all over [the edge]. Because at that point we knew we were okay, but we never thought we really were good until then. Especially coming from him when he didn't throw compliments around."

Sutton always maintained the 26-2 team of 1976-77 that went undefeated in the SWC was as good or better than the 32-4 team of 1977-78. It's just that those 1976-77 Hogs didn't know how good they were, and it manifested in losing a big lead with the first-round jitters during their first-round NCAA Tourney loss to Wake Forest.

"We just didn't have the confidence," Moncrief said.

They would get that confidence in the 1978 NCAA Tourney in beating UCLA, not far removed from the incomparable John Wooden era.

"We were not known to most of the United States," Moncrief said, "and UCLA was a powerhouse. That ballgame was probably the biggest in my career—that game and Houston. When Houston was first inaugurated into the Southwest Conference and we beat them, 92-47. Those two games helped prepare Arkansas for national prominence."

Mutual Respect

The Triplets—all old high school rivals with Brewer graduating from Fort Smith Northside and Delph from Conway in 1974, and Moncrief from Little Rock Hall in 1975—bantered and teased each other throughout their Razorback tenure. But they truly bonded in mutual respect.

"I didn't care if Ron got the headline," Moncrief told Stan Heath's Razorbacks at their 2004 postseason banquet, "or Marvin got more points. I didn't care about anything but going out there and spanking some—whatever. That's all we cared about."

Because of his legendary intensity, and as the lone remaining Triplet in 1979 carrying the Razorbacks on his back all the way to the Elite Eight and a tremendous down-to-the-wire game with Larry Bird and Indiana State, Moncrief generally gets recalled as the greatest Triplet. Most considered his lone rival to the honor of "greatest Razorback ever" to be Corliss Williamson.

But Delph was the Triplet's greatest shooter, and for Sidney's money, Brewer the best overall player.

"I had the opportunity to play with no doubt the greatest athletic talent in Arkansas history," Moncrief told the banquet. "Ron Brewer."

If the Shoe Fits...

ESPN sportscaster Jimmy Dykes occasionally was seen playing a basketball game instead of describing one.

That was back in the 1980s when Dykes was a walk-on reserve guard for Eddie Sutton's Razorbacks. Dykes played in brief mop-up appearances, usually coinciding with the band itching to pack up the tubas while janitors were breaking out the buckets and brooms because so few fans were left to impede the cleanup.

One day that role seemed certain to change.

"Robert Kitchen, the backup point guard, was hurt or suspended or something," Dykes recalled. "Whatever, we were playing Texas A&M, and he wasn't going to play. I figured I was the third point guard behind Ricky Norton and Robert Kitchen. With Kitchen out, I thought I almost had to play."

Surely by the second half, Norton would need a breather.

"But Ricky just kept going," Dykes said. "He didn't get tired, and he didn't get in foul trouble. But with about eight minutes left he suddenly starts hobbling around."

Dykes looked exhilarated.

"I didn't want him to get hurt," Dykes said. "But I am thinking, 'I am going to PLAY!' And sure enough, they call me up by Coach Sutton. I look out and there's still a crowd!

Then I hear Coach Sutton ask, 'What's your shoe size?' I tell him 10 1/2 and I hear, 'That will fit. Take off your left shoe!'"

Dykes sighed.

"Ricky blew out a shoe," Dykes said. "They wanted mine. So instead of playing, I'm on the bench the rest of the game with one shoe on and one shoe off."

Brick by Brick

The late Steve Stroud, a strong defensive but definitely not offensively oriented center both for Lanny Van Eman and Eddie Sutton, was a Razorback with a sharp dry wit, but every once in a while would get zinged himself.

"We were going to play Texas Tech and were coming into Lubbock Coliseum," former Razorback trainer Mike McDonald recalled. "We walk in and there are a bunch of bricks and somebody yells, 'Hey, Stroud, looks like they've stacked up all your shots!'"

Remembered in Missouri 20 Years Later

You wouldn't think Charles Balentine's game-winning shot to beat top-ranked North Carolina, 65-64 in Pine Bluff in 1984 would still resonate at all up in Missouri. But it does, Balentine has learned as district manager overseeing seven WalMart stores in the Springfield-Joplin surrounding areas.

"If they hear my name when they page me in a WalMart store," Balentine said, "people will come up and say, 'Are you the guy?' ... And I just say, 'Yeah.' I was amazed to see how many Arkansas fans live in Missouri."

Must have made for some lively discussions before Arkansas's football team beat Missouri in the 2003 Independence Bowl.

"Oh, yeah," Balentine said. "I had a lot of bets with my store managers, because I knew we were going to win. So now there are a lot of store managers wearing Razorback hats."

Like Scotty Thurman's shot off a hurried, fumbling Dwight Stewart pass that buried Duke in Arkansas's national championship basketball victory over Duke in 1994, Balentine's game-winner was not game-planned.

"I was the third or fourth option in the whole deal," Balentine said. "I wasn't supposed to be getting the ball in that time frame when Alvin Robertson passed it. I just happen to be closer to Alvin for him to get the ball to me. It was a sharp pass because he had to get rid of it, and I was just fortunate enough to be close and put it in. There were exactly five seconds left. It was a great feeling for our basketball team and the state of Arkansas. It really gave us a lot notoriety for that whole year. We were playing against a powerful team. Michael Jordan, Sam Perkins, Brad Daugherty and Steve Hale were on that team."

Appreciating Eddie's Culture

Some of Balentine's most lasting basketball team experiences had nothing to do with basketball, he said.

"Coach Sutton used to take us to museums, art shows and meet famous people," Balentine said. "And we would wonder, 'Why is he doing this?' And he would tell us, 'You need to learn this stuff, because you never know when you'll have to be involved in this one day.' Years later I understand why he did it. And we don't do that enough with players now, show them the business and the cultural side. Because not everybody is going to make it in the NBA. Those are things that athletes need to know."

It helps those who made the NBA, too. Darrell Walker, still an NBA scout after retiring as a longtime NBA player, is one of the most avid art collectors in Arkansas.

Excitement Not Shared

H ere's a twist on an Aggie joke.
How many Razorbacks in Aggie country does it take to celebrate a Hogs victory over Texas A&M in College Station?

The answer, Joe Kleine knows, is none. Because Joe said he proved one is one too many. Kleine was celebrating in street-clothes as a redshirting transfer from Notre Dame when Eddie Sutton's 1982 basketball Razorbacks came back to beat the Aggies, 64-63 at G. Rollie White Coliseum.

"We won, and I was going crazy," Kleine said. "I was running off the court, and I thought I had left my jacket, the only sportscoat I had to my name, on the bench. I turned around to get it and realized I had it on. Everyone had gone to our locker room and I thought, 'Woops! Better get out of town.' We had been getting drilled the whole game and then we came back late. Darrell Walker of all people won it with one of his pure knuckleball strokes."

An Altar Boy's Big Blessing

D uring his induction into the University of Arkansas's Sports Hall of Honor, Joe Kleine, the past several years the colorman on Razorback basketball broadcasts, talked both of his late father and the blessing of coming home to Arkansas after 15 seasons in the NBA.

"I lost my dad to leukemia after my rookie year," Kleine said. "He showed me God by example. Getting up to mass every day and taking me with him. There were times Slater, Missouri had the tallest altar boy ever. I was 6-11, and the altar boy did-n't show up and my dad tapped me on the shoulder and said, 'Get up there.' So I'd stand up there and nobody could see the priest. There was just this little voice there coming out from behind me."

Joe said he's always felt blessed, particularly when he transferred from Notre Dame after his freshman year to Arkansas.

"If somebody asked me," Kleine said, "what's the smartest thing you ever did? I would say it was leaving Notre Dame to come to the University of Arkansas. The best thing I ever did in my life.

"It came down to Arkansas and Notre Dame and I chose Door No. 2 when I should have chosen Door No. 1. But that wasn't my final answer. I should have used my lifeline."

Cheap Thug over Unemployed Star

Former Razorback All-Southwest Conference basketball star Scott Hastings knew in a hurry he must make more out of less if he was going to last in the NBA.

"When I played at Arkansas, I always felt I was a pretty good player, an offensive player," said Hastings, a starting center from 1979-82, for Eddie Sutton's Razorbacks. "My last year in college I averaged 18 points. But I started talking to coaches and general managers around the league, and they thought at Arkansas I was a soft player. When I left the league, I was basically known as a thug. I don't exactly know when the transformation happened. But you are always going to need someone who is solid defensively, rebounds and does the little things. I had always been fundamentally sound in those areas, and I realized I wasn't going to average those 18 to 20 points in the pros. But I could have a long career doing the little things in the pros. Making an inbound pass with :04 on the clock when they needed it inbounded, or playing defense on Hakeem Olajuwon. I had an edge on [Olajuwon], because I played against him in college and I knew how good he really was."

Hastings's most famous Razorback shot is a buzzer beater to beat a great Houston Phi Slama Jama team. Olajuwon, then called Akeem rather than Hakeem, came out of nowhere and nearly blocked it.

"My grandma had a picture of that," Hastings said. "The ball is above Olajuwon's hand just about an inch."

All-Quote Team

A Scott Hastings quote when he joined a then first-year Miami Heat franchise after being an Atlanta Hawk for five years likely started his post NBA career in sportscasting. He now lives in Denver doing radio for both the Broncos and the Nuggets.

"I'm one of the best players here," Hastings was quoted at Miami. "And that scares the hell out of me!"

The quote got national play.

"It was true," Hastings said of the fledgling Heat. "That was a bad team. But I'm proud of that team, because we were all pretty close. We all sucked to be honest with you."

It wasn't the only quote that made Hastings the most quoted NBA benchwarmer of his time. Hastings said he got named to some NBA "All-Quote teams."

"I was pretty proud of that," Hastings said, "considering that guys like Charles Barkley and Karl Malone were on it."

Eddie's Advice

H astings said heeding Eddie Sutton's advice helped his NBA shelf life.

"I remember," Hastings said, "Eddie Sutton saying, 'If you apply yourself, you can have a long career. Play 10 years and you have it made. I lasted 11 years but I don't have it made. I would like to have those 11 years, now even if I didn't get to play any more than I got to play. Minimum salary is $1 million. I would like to make $1 million for 11 years."

He must have been making close to $1 million by the end.

"No," Hastings said, "that's where I fool people. I had a philosophy, no job is too small. And if you overprice yourself, you might not play.

"The last I looked, it was still minimum wage sacking groceries. The minimum when I played was $150,000. Where else am I going to make $150,000? So the thing I did was try and not overprice myself."

Who Was that Masked Man?

Scott Hastings also offered a tidbit on Keith Burns, the former defensive coordinator for Houston Nutt's Razorbacks and a Razorback football player when Hastings was a Hog.

"I know secrets about Keith Burns that Keith doesn't want me to tell," Hastings said. "I still have pictures of Keith. He and Billy Ray Smith used to wear this mask, and they'd put on a toga that looked like a diaper and run through the sorority houses and fraternity parties."

Any other UA memories to relate?

"I don't think so," Hastings said, "because youngsters will be reading this. I want them to do as I say, not as I did. As you get older, you appreciate the time you spend in college. I appreciate that more than ever, and I miss it. It's a wonderful time of life. I wish I had could do it over and still have the knowledge I have now. I would have appreciated the game in the regional finals against Indiana State (and Larry Bird) a little more. And I would have appreciated the game in Dallas that ended our senior year. I would change a lot of things but I still would go to Maxine's whenever I could."

Maxine's is a beer bar still operating in Fayetteville after 50 plus years.

A Sleeper's Nightmare

As one of the fabled Triplets with Ron Brewer and Sidney Moncrief, Marvin Delph enjoyed many a legendary moment with Eddie Sutton's Razorbacks.

One of the most legendary, Marvin recalled with one of those Marvin smiles that could light up a cave, was off the court and didn't involve.

It instead involved Dan Pauley, a center Eddie endured for one year after inheriting him from Lanny Van Eman.

"The day after every game," Delph recalled, "Coach Sutton was going to watch game film. We got beat, just gave the game away, so Coach Sutton was in a bad mood, anyway. Dan Pauley was sitting in the first row. Coach Sutton turned the lights back on, and Pauley was asleep, snoring. You know how Coach Sutton could get on somebody. He scalded him. The devil couldn't have come up with more words than Coach Sutton came up with that day. If I didn't have the fear of God in me before, I had it that day."

So did others, even if they weren't there and were just told about it.

Marvin said Sidney Moncrief, who joined the Hogs out of Little Rock Hall a year after Delph had signed out of Conway, knew all about Dan's dozing.

"I remember," Delph said, "Sidney asked, 'Does Coach Sutton always act like that when somebody messes up?'

"I just told him, 'Don't go to sleep! I don't care if you need pins in your eyes to keep them open, don't go to sleep!'"

Shrinking that Swelled Head

Though Delph was a gunner playing for a coach who doted on defense, he fit in beautifully with Sutton's system.

Marvin fit in, he said, thanks to a lesson learned in Conway High School from Coach Herman Lasker.

"In high school I got the big head," Delph said. "The second day of my senior year I quit the team. My coach was wanting me to run the offense, and I told him, 'The only offense you need is me.' Coach Herman Lasker sat me down and told me how how the cow ate the cabbage. He intervened when I needed direction. He saved my career."

Revising Sutton's 3 Ds

Even on the backs of the Razorbacks' practice uniforms, Eddie Sutton always emphasized the Three Ds of Dedication, Discipine and Defense. Delph always wanted to amend that third D.

"I always said," Marvins said smiling, "the Three Ds were Dedication, Discipline and Delph. I remember Coach Sutton in practice shouting, 'Delph, you couldn't cover my grandmother. And she's dead!'"

Putting His Finger on the Pulse

Back in 1975, Arkansas center Daryll Saulsberry recalled Texas Tech center Rick Bullock putting his finger on the Barnhill Arena madness as Bullock fouled out during a Razorback victory.

"I remember Bullock walking out flipping everybody off," Saulsberry said. "That takes nerve. Not a whole lot of class—but it does take nerve."

Dave Woodman, the Razorbacks' radio play by play man at the time, described Bullock's exit thusly: "He's making a gesture—it's the worst one you can think of!"

All My Exes Live in Texas

All-time leading Razorback scorer Todd Day played for three Nolan Richardson-coached Southwest Conference championship teams and finished on Richardson's first Southeastern Conference championship team.

Day said it was exciting to win Arkansas's SEC debut, yet it lacked something from the previous three.

"The one thing we miss moving to the SEC is the Texas rivalry," Day said. "People to this day don't like Texas even though we aren't in the same conference. It was a fierce battle. They were always ranked and we were always ranked. Sweet Tom is the coach I remembered most."

"Sweet Tom" was Richardson's moniker for former Texas coach Tom Penders.

Richardson was most sour about "Sweet Tom" when the Razorbacks were making their second swing through the SWC schedule and were in Austin trying to complete a home-and-home sweep. An article in the *Austin American Statesman* greeted Richardson with Penders claiming film showed over 20 bad calls against Texas in Fayetteville. Penders would bring that to the officials' attention.

Richardson fumed, especially with Texas leading late and some calls appearing to the Arkansas coach like they were made through burnt orange-colored glasses.

"The sweetest moment was when Nolan walked off the floor," Day said, "and came back and we ended up winning in overtime. That really set Tom off. I had fouled out of the game and was sitting right there and Nolan got up and said, 'I can't take it anymore,' and stormed off. I didn't know where he was going at the time."

Assistant coach Scott Edgar was running the team when Lee Mayberry hit the miracle three to tie it and send it to the overtime that brought Richardson out of the locker room. Arkansas won handily, 103-96.

The Hogs returned that year to Austin to edge Princeton, 68-64 and Dayton, 68-64 in the first two rounds of the NCAA Tournament to advance to Dallas and rout North Carolina, 96-73 and play Texas again.

"Beating Texas (88-85) and North Carolina to advance to the Final Four was the sweetest," Day said. "I hit a jumper at the buzzer to beat Dayton. Princeton—that was a tough game. That was the first time we had seen a slowdown in almost a year."

Out of Thin Air

Day said the Razorbacks underestimated the mile-high altitude with their all-out press that ran out of gas in a 97-83 Final Four semifinal loss to Duke.

"We weren't as deep as we were the following year," Day said, "and relied mainly on seven or eight. Fatigue was really a factor. We were up 11 towards the end of the half and even into the second half when fatigue took over. We were still trying to press and nobody had legs and they ended up having easy shots."

You Can Go Home Again

A brand new Day came home to Arkansas in November, 2002, after a long NBA career to be inducted into the UA Sports Hall of Honor and then the following semester became a UA student working on completing his degree that he understandably had put off. Media, loving to watch Day but loathing to interview the often petulant, temperamental player in his Razorback playing days, were shocked with his Hall of Honor speech and demeanor.

Todd Day—shown here in his days as a star forward for Arkansas—returned to the university in 2002 to be inducted into the UA Sports Hall of Honor.

The change seems to continue. For that he credits his wife, Brenda, a schoolteacher, and time.

"I think I'm a lot more mature than I was then," Day said. "Time makes you change your perspective of life. I know what I have to do now, and I was a kid at that point."

The Hall of Honor induction was truly poignant, not just for his speech, one of the best delivered since the event began, but to see him listen intently and applaud the other honorees' speeches. Watching him drink in all it is to be Razorback not just for him, but the others, was a sight to behold, and lightyears removed from how he seemed when he played here.

"I definitely enjoyed my four years," Day said. "I think it definitely helped me with the NBA to have been in this type of atmosphere, always being in the limelight. It gets you used to that next level and being a quote—star—unquote. It was very gratifying for me to tell everybody I came from the University of Arkansas and I'm proud like every athlete that has ever played here. It was a time I had to show my gratitude for everything people had done for me while I was here. You never really have a chance to tell them. I just took it as my moment to let people know how much I appreciated their help through the good and bad times I was here. It took me two or three weeks to get the speech prepared because I really wanted to say all the right things. My family really enjoyed hearing about me playing here and getting to see the pictures and plaques and old game film. I think my family was probably more excited than I was."

Standing Pat on Walton Arena

Before coming back to the University of Arkansas to graduate, Pat Bradley knocked around the country playing pro basketball in some minor leagues.

The career SEC three-point leader during his 1995-96 through 1998-99 tenure for Nolan Richardson's Razorbacks learned fast there is no way professionally—on any level—he believes to recapture the excitement of playing in Walton Arena.

"It would be tough to find NBA arenas with that kind of electricity," Bradley said. "The college atmosphere is unique anyway. College sports is really about the team spirit. You play

15 games at Walton and everyone of them is juiced, especially in the SEC. At the SEC Tournament in Atlanta my senior year, the night before we played I watched an NBA game. It was ridiculous. Nobody cared. They weren't even paying attention to the game. People root for the college. Coach Richardson kept saying, 'The Razorbacks would always be here. That the players change but the Razorbacks don't. They fill the seats to root for the Razorbacks. Regardless of who is on the court, they love the Razorbacks.'"

Count Bradley among them. He says he's "blessed" to have been a Razorback. And he says Richardson blessed him by making him become as complete a player as his skills would allow to go with his great perimeter shot.

"I hated being known as a specialist or three-point shooter," Bradley said. "I wanted to be known as a basketball player who could shoot. I didn't like the labels. I always knew I could do a little more than just shoot, and so did Coach. Sometimes when my shot wasn't going down, you knew there was something else you could give the team, something they needed. That's when you would take a look at what else can I do to help? Any situation you're put in, you've got to try and make the best of it. That's for sure.'"

Language Barrier

Even if his travels take him to Europe or the Orient, the Everett, Massachusettes native won't face the language barrier he first faced speaking "Bahston" to "Arkansaw" and viceversa.

Bradley laughed.

"That was fun," Bradley said. "I think if I was from Texas or Missouri, it wouldn't have been what it was. It was the whole idea of coming halfway across the country. People still say, 'Say something, I want to hear you talk.' I think the whole idea of being unknown caught people's attention, but fitting in here wasn't tough to do at all. Though it made for a good, good story. If I didn't come to school here, it would have been very, very different. It was a special blessing to come here, not only play but experience an area like this. Some of the greatest people I know are down here."

Recruiting a Second God

B radley's Massachusetts accent became one of Nolan Richardson's banquet story staples.

"I'm recruiting this guy who calls himself a god," Richardson said. "I said, "a god?!' He'd say, yeah, yeah, a 2-god."

Richardson quickly adapted to the New England difference between god and "gahd."

Early Memories

W hat does Bradley remember most of his Hog days? "Funny as it sounds," Bradley said, "the things I remember most are the practices. The running, getting up at 4:45 in the morning to get to the morning practice. That sticks with you. And the tournament games stick with you. That's when the hype is there. And my last game at Bud Walton when we played Auburn, you know going into it what the game is. Now that Sweet Sixteen team when I was a freshman was an incredible experience. Especially going back to Providence. There were probably a couple of hundred from Everett at the game. I didn't know what to expect. We kept playing and winning and having fun. We were so young and innocent and that was the happiest time. Sometimes you don't know the great games are great until the game is over. But the last game at Bud Walton, you do."

Taking One for the Team

Roger Crawford was an excellent, versatile reserve guard-small forward for Nolan Richardson's 1994 national champions.

However when it came to taking charges, Crawford cashed no credit.

Except once.

Richardson remembered the time when the spindly Crawford took a charge worthy of that team's chief charge-taker, stocky guard Corey Beck.

A mammoth power forward was driving, Richardson recalled. Crawford stood his ground before flying into the nickel seats.

Richardson and the Razorback bench erupted with high-fives as the referee called a charge.

"Way to go, son!" Richardson shouted as he clapped the woozy Crawford on the back and sent in a substitute. "You finally took a charge!"

"So that's what happened?" Crawford replied according to Richardson. "Man, I just couldn't get out of the way."

Crawford played a key reserve role for the Razorbacks' 1994 national championship team but actually earned his most fame after he was injured during the tournaments. The Razorbacks wore patches with No. 31, Crawford's uniform number, during the tournament.

And when they won it, Crawford, cast and all, was sitting on top of the basket during the postgame net-cutting ceremonies.

Sweeping to a National Championship

For a book called *The 1994 National Champions* I co-authored with Dudley Dawson, then of the *Northwest Arkansas Times*, Scotty Thurman credited a broomstick for his historic three-pointer with 51 seconds left in Arkansas's NCAA Championship victory over Duke.

The 6-5 Thurman snapped a 70-70 tie and sealed Duke's fate in Arkansas's 76-72 national championship victory launching a three over 6-8 Duke defender Antonio Lang with the game clock at 51 seconds and the shot clock winding to naught.

"That broomstick thing helped me a lot," Thurman said. "My high school coach had me shooting over a broomstick in the summer because he told me in college I'd have to shoot over taller people."

A taller foe and the shortest shot clock.

"I had no choice but to put it up," Thurman said.

Thurman's shot swept Lang away.

"It was a big-time shot," Lang said. "I don't know how he made it. I had a hand in his face, and the ball was an inch away from my finger."

Coach Nolan Richardson, who had likened Thurman's shooting range as "from wherever he comes into the gym," called it "the best shot I have ever seen."

Arkansas point guard Corey Beck observed, "Scotty stepped up like the Thurminator."

Smarter than the Brilliant

Before Arkansas played Duke for the 1994 national championship, there was much national media ado about Duke being the "smart team," which implied without saying it that Arkansas was the dumb team.

Corliss Williamson was no dummy when it came to beating Duke in the '94 championship game.

Corliss Williamson, Arkansas's stronger than strong, 6-7, 245-pound forward rebutted with convincing simplicity at the pre-championship game press conference.

"If you have a little, smart guy," Williamson said, "and a big, tough dumb guy, and they are in a fight—who do you think is going to win?"

Corliss, still playing well in the NBA as the Detroit Pistons' sixth man, was and is no dummy. He sure was too tough, and too smart for Duke as his game-high 23 points paced the Razorbacks' 76-72 national championship triumph.

Corlissville

Only Sidney Moncrief's Razorback days in the 1970s before or since rivaled the statewide basketball popularity hold that Corliss Williamson held on Arkansas. From 1992-94, "Big Nasty" reigned supreme in the state while leading Nolan Richardson's Razorbacks to the Sweet Sixteen, national championship and national runnerup.

In fact, Williamson one-upped Moncrief in one aspect. No Arkansas city ever changed its name in honor of Little Rock native Moncrief. Russellville, Williamson's home town, officially changed its name to "Corlissville" for the day it honored its hometown hero.

Even the *Arkansas Democrat-Gazette* dateline for Bob Holt's story was "CORLISSVILLE" when Williamson was honored.

Nolan's Pet Secret

Razorback fans loved Wabbaseka's Ernie Murry, the friendliest basketball walk-on since Eugene Nash played for Eddie Sutton in the 1970s and early '80s.

Nolan Richardson loved him, too, but the now former Arkansas coach seldom showed it until Murry's career was over. That's because Ernie wasn't just a friendly walk-on but a good one, good enough to be Arkansas's best player in the game when a team including Lee Mayberry, Todd Day and Oliver Miller lost in the 1991 NCAA Midwest Regional final to Kansas.

"One thing I'll never forget," Murry said, "is to hear Coach Richardson say how it went for me as a walk-on was one of the greatest things he ever had in coaching. I was treated just as well as the scholarship players. I have the greatest respect for Coach Richardson and the University. He's a great guy who cares about his players and his ex-players."

Ernie acknowledged he wasn't hearing great things from the coach when he reported back his senior year. Murry had a fan favorite upon being being a junior college transfer from Mississippi County JC.

"He thought I was the fans' pet and talking to the media too much," Murry said. "He said I came back my senior year full, overweight. So I had to work hard again."

It was hard keeping his weight down at the UA, considering how his life had been previously at Mississippi County Junior College.

"One thing I remember from junior college—everything was a bus riding seven hours," Murry said. "Here it was fly everywhere. Junior college you had one good meal a day. Arkansas was three squares with a variety. Junior college you had two pair of tennis shoes for the whole year. At Arkansas you'd get two a month. I will always be loyal to this program. Every time I come up here, I tell people I'm going home."

Separating Elite Eight from Final Four

Ernie Murry has two words that separated the 1991 Razorbacks not going to the Final Four, even with stars Lee Mayberry, Todd Day and Oliver Miller as sophomores, after making the 1990 Final Four: Lenzie Howell. Howell, was the 6-4 senior unsung hero of the 1989 and '90 Razorback Southwest Conference championship teams.

"Lenzie Howell was in the shadow of three great guys," Murry said. "But you look at those games, he was BIG. He'd always get the stickback. That Texas game, he played great. Lenzie went on and played in Holland, he may still be over there. My senior year we didn't have the guy who could go get you that rebound in traffic and go back up and put in and get you the bucket and one. We needed a 'tweener my senior year. We didn't have that type of player in '91 who could get the 6-7 player and guard him and get the 6-3 player and guard him."

An Arkie of a Different Stripe

Once revered as a Razorback in Arkansas, and still looked upon admirably as a counselor for at risk students in Pine Bluff, Ernie now finds himself booed in his home state when he performs his second job.

Murry moonlights as a basketball official working some college and high school games.

"The pressure on these college coaches to win is unbelievable," Murry said. "When you are the visiting coach, you walk into the gym thinking you are screwed. They've got the crowd, they got the clock operator. I played college basketball. I knew some guys on the road, and everything was a foul. Those same guys, when they jumped on a plane and came to Fayetteville, you could murder people. I think people sometimes get caught up."

Don Rutledge, now retired, was the best college official he ever saw, Ernie says.

"He's the same guy no matter what," Murry said, recalling a Nolan Richardson-Rick Pitino-Rutledge incident. "I remember an Arkansas-Kentucky game a few years ago that we had a screwy clock situation. Pitino is going nuts. And Nolan is going nuts. So Rutledge brings them together, and they both are screaming, and Rutledge says, 'Other than that screwup, how are we doing?' They said, 'Fine.' He said, 'Let's play ball.'

"A guy like that can do that. He is one of the best there is. He doesn't have a quick T. He takes a lot and knows how to handle himself. He's a class guy. If you can't call with him, something is wrong with you. He makes it so simple."

England Remembers

Serving Razorback basketball coaches from Eddie Sutton to Stan Heath, veteran trainer David England recalls guard

Corey Beck (1993-95) and forward Derek Hood (1996-99) as the toughest Hog hoopsters.

"I remember when we were in Hawaii at the Rainbow Classic," England said, "and the team went swimming in the Ocean. There was some coral and Corey Beck says, I cut my foot. We take him to the doctor and he gets 20-something stitches in the arch of his foot.

"The doctor says, 'Sorry, you aren't going to be able to play in this tournament.' Corey kind of winks at me. He ends up playing all but two minutes for the three games in the tournament with 20 stitches in the bottom of his foot. He and Derek Hood were the two toughest. Derek would dive into anything for a ball. He was unbelievable."

The Nolan Era

The harsh parting between Nolan Richardson and the University of Arkansas, closing with a lawsuit tried two seasons after he had last coached, left a bitterly divisive conclusion to the Razorbacks' most glorious basketball era. Obviously there wasn't much laughter at the end, but there was plenty to smile about with Nolan when times were good and even during some bad times, too.

Here are some reminders that things weren't always acrimonious.

Nolan and Names

Nolan Richardson won more games and probably lost more names than any Razorback basketball coach. Arkansas's former coach rivals legendary New York Yankee manager Casey Stengel for botching or just completely forgetting names.

Terry Mercer, the UA longtime basketball secretary to Eddie Sutton, Richardson and now Stan Heath, always took pains to write in all names for Richardson before the coaches made introductions at the annual basketball banquet.

On one occasion connections were missed.

After some Paul Harvey-length pauses, Nolan introduced, "My secretary, Terry Mercer, and her husband—Mercer. My assistant coach, Mike Anderson and his wife—Marcheita—and daugher Darcheita—and all the other Cheitas. My assistant coach, Brad Dunn. And his wife—Mrs. Dunn."

Your author once was part of Nolan's name gaffes.

When using media as honorary "coaches" for a Red-White game, Nolan announced to the crowd, "Paul Eells and Mike Nail will coach the Red team. And coaching the White team, Orville Henry and Nate—the Skate."

My wife, Nancy, still refers to herself as Mrs. Skate.

Of course even she was less bemused than Blake Eddins, the Razorback Richardson once called "Ed Blakins."

Not that Nolan was alone in forgetting names. Under Lou Holtz, Razorback outside linebacker Mark Lee finally just started answering to Brad as Lou was far more apt to call him Brad Lee than Mark Lee.

Can't Beat That

Nolan didn't have much cause to laugh at himself while compiling the best record of any UA head basketball coach, but he did nail himself with a deprecating joke as the first Hog team he inherited from Eddie Sutton struggled to 12-16 in 1985-86.

"A little boy was in court," Nolan related, "and the little boy said, "I can't stay with my mother anymore. She beats me."

"Well," the judge said, "then we'll rule that you will live with your father."

"I don't want to go with him," the little boy said. "He beats me, too."

"Well," the judge said, "If you don't want to live with your father and you don't want to live with your mother, then who do you want to live with?"

"Nolan Richardson," the boy replied. "He doesn't beat anybody."

Blind Luck

Dick Vitale's schtick always was okay with Nolan Richardson, but the Arkansas coach could never much abide CBS's Billy Packer. Postgame during a national telecast, Packer pontificated a question to Nolan that sounded more like a statement of the obvious.

"A blind man could see that, Billy," Nolan replied.

It's All There in Black and White

During his days coaching the University of Tulsa, Richardson became famous for his polka-dot shirts. He started wearing them, he said, because his friend, Tulsa clothier Ed Beshara, had a bunch of polka-dot shirts that never sold.

On a lark, Nolan wore one for a home game, and TU won. He wore a coat and tie for the next game, a road game, and TU lost.

"At midnight I get a call from a little, old lady," Nolan said. "She asked me, 'Do you know why you lost?'

"'No, why?'

"'It's because you didn't wear your polka dots.'"

So Nolan started wearing them home and road, and they became a trend around Tulsa.

"I'm going to the store," Nolan said, "and I'm shopping and this little lady comes up to me and asks, 'How much money do you make?'

"And I said, 'I make a pretty good living.'

"And she says, 'Then you need to buy some more polka-dot shirts. Because I'm tired of looking at the black and white one all the time.'

"I said, 'I've got black and white, red and white, blue and white. I've got all kinds of polka dots.'

"'No you don't,' she said, 'Every game I see on TV you're wearing that black and white one.'"

Seems she had a black-and-white TV, Nolan learned.

"I assured her," Nolan said. "'I do have different colors, ma'am.'"

Booooo!

During the 2001-2002 basketball season, referee Ted Hillary became the most marked man in Arkansas—for a while. A month later, Hillary could have sneaked unnoticed into Walton Arena. Fans would have been too busy booing UA marketing director Matt Shanklin.

Hillary became nationally infamous to Razorback basketball fans because in an eyebrow-raising call on ESPN national television, he disallowed in Chicago the go-ahead basket by Arkansas's Brandon Dean with a charging call as 5.5 seconds remained against then nationally fifth-ranked Illinois.

With Dean's basket disallowed, and Illinois instead shooting free throws, the Illini prevailed.

Even ESPN's impartial announcers questioned the call.

That was December 8, 2001. On January 8, Shanklin eclipsed Hillary for one night on the unpopularity meter.

It was halftime during Arkansas's SEC victory over Mississippi State at Walton Arena. Shanklin oversaw a contest sponsored by Fuji Photo. Make a layup and then a three-point-er and it qualified the contestant, 22-year-old UA student Michael Collyer, for a halfcourt shot worth $10,000.

Collyer made the layup and swished the three.

Suspense built. He launched the halfcourt shot. In it went to a thunderous ovation.

Collyer leaped about, celebrating. Then he slumped in shock.

Shanklin detected that Collyer was several inches past the midcourt line when he let fly. Not valid, he ruled.

The crowd booed. They booed so loudly that reporters back in the closed-door press room trying to write at halftime scrambled out wondering if somehow the second half had begun early.

The booing crowd didn't know Shanklin's motive. The insurance company that would have actually paid the $10,000 wouldn't pay if its adjusters saw film of Collyer shooting over the line. A man in the crowd knew that, too. Didn't matter. He waved his arms in a public frenzy.

"Boooo!" Arkansas athletic director Frank Broyles yelled in his unmistakable Georgia accent. "That's awful! That's terrible! It's a PR nightmare! A PR nightmare!"

Not quite as vociferous, but sharing the same opinion, was UA Chancellor Dr. John White.

They cornered Shanklin who would have been booed even had he ducked into a church.

Collyer's shot was declared good to the crowd's roaring approval. It was paid for by the Razorback Foundation.

A full week later this writer chanced upon Shanklin at the Broyles Complex.

"Booo!" the writer said.

It was only the eighth boo Shanklin heard that day before noon.

"Aw, geez," Shanklin replied. "Are you all ever going to let me live that down?"

Sweet Charlotte Gets Peeved

When Nolan Richardson's 1994 Razorbacks beat Duke to win the national championship in Charlotte, Arkansas fans in the Charlotte Coliseum called the Hogs and hugged, and called the Hogs and hugged, and called the Hogs and hugged ...

Finally, a genteel, Southern woman's voice over the Coliseum's public address system said, "Charlotte, has enjoyed hosting the tournament, but it's time to go."

Fans paused to hear the announcement. Somebody called the Hogs. It was back to hugging and whooping and mass Hog calling.

Again came the voice, slightly less genteel but still velvet, "Charlotte has enjoyed hosting the tournament, but it's time to go."

A pause, then more Hog calling and hugging.

Two more announcements, each testier and moving up the Mason Dixon line.

"Charlotte has enjoyed hosting the tournament ..."

The last announcement sounded like a Brooklyn transmit cop ejecting a panhandler off the subway.

"We're shutting it down. Get outta here!"

Who knows what might have been said next.

The fans I talked with didn't tarry to find out.

Eddins Still Hits the Mark

Blake Eddins's jumpshot deserted him his last couple of Razorback seasons, but his quips never failed to miss the mark. That's why after coaching the Razorbacks for his first season, Stan Heath asked Eddins to address the team banquet to represent the other five seniors Heath inherited from former Razorback coach Nolan Richardson.

Eddins immediately poked loving fun at Heath, maybe the most organized coach in college basketball.

"Everyone knows Coach is a real scheduled guy," Eddins said. "When his kids get up in the morning they have a meeting. Then they have a meeting before they go to school. And a meeting going out the door. A meeting when they come home. Then they have a meeting to talk about that meeting."

A Really Cool Trainer

B asketball trainer David England was always cool in how he handled treating bruises, Eddins said.

"He'll put you in icewater in the whirlpool," Eddins said. "Amble back in 20 minutes later and put in another bucket of ice and kind of laugh."

No. 1 at No. 6

E ddins marveled about Arkansas surpassing 15,000 in attendance average to be second in SEC attendance only to league-champion Kentucky playing in 24,000-seat Rupp Arena.

Pretty impressive for a team that went 9-19 in 2002-2003.

"We have the best fans in the country," Eddins said. "Alabama was ranked No. 1 in the country (in December and drawing 6,000 or 7,000 and we were sixth in the SEC (West) and drawing 15,500."

Boyer, Old Boy

After Tommy Boyer, a Razorback from 1961-63 and a prominent businessman and generous UA booster, gave the keynote address on academics in athletics at the banquet, Eddins remarked about the six seniors who played from freshmen through juniors for Richardson and their senior year for Heath.

"You've got six guys who are doing something that probably hasn't been done since Tommy Boyer played here," Eddins said. "Though I'm not sure if they gave out diplomas back then."

With Heath, then 38, and athletic director Frank Broyles, then 78, attending, Eddins fancied his life as an about-to-be alum.

"I look forward to coming back in 20 years," Eddins said, "with Coach Heath here and Coach Broyles still the AD."

Sorry, Wrong Number

Alabama-born, Auburn-bred Blake Eddins got an Arkansas history lesson by the numbers upon signing with the Razorbacks.

Eddins was going to walk on at Auburn until former Arkansas coach Nolan Richardson offered him a scholarship. Richardson liked what he saw during a Nike summer camp after Blake had already graduated from high school.

"Here I'm thinking I'm going to be a walk-on at Auburn," Eddins said. "And Coach Richardson is offering me a scholarship and telling me how much he wants me. I don't know anything about Arkansas, but Coach Richardson and Coach [Mike] Anderson were saying how important I could be. I get up here and they ask, 'What number do you want?'"

Eddins paused.

It took Blake Eddins a laundry list of numbers—and a history les-son—to settle on jersey No. 21.

"Now I'm really excited," Eddins said. "I'm thinking, I really must be important to them. They're asking me what number do I want?'"

He had no clue how fast he'd devalue in the numbers game.

"I first asked for No. 24," Eddins said. "And they said, 'No, Joe Johnson (a fellow incoming freshman battling academic ineligibilty then and playing in the NBA two years later) is going to have that.'

"I said, 'But he's not even eligible this semester,' but they said, 'That's a special deal. Now, what other number would you like?'

"'How about 32?'

"They laughed. 'This boy is funny. That's Sidney's number and it's retired.'"

Sidney Moncrief is forever Sidney in Arkansas lore.

"'OK, how about 34?'

"'That's Corliss's number. You can't have that.'"

Corliss Williamson also doesn't need his last name to be identified in Arkansas.

"'But it's not retired, is it?'

"'You can't have it. Try another one.'

"'No. 30?'

"'That's Scotty's number? You can't have Scotty Thurman's number.'

"'How about 14?'

"'That's Corey Beck.'"

Eddins sighed.

"I finally got No. 2, but changed it to No. 21."

Heath Bars and Hog Calls

When now-former Kent State head coach Stan Heath was announced as Arkansas's new head basketball on March

Razorback coach Stan Heath had a thing or two to learn about Hog calls upon getting the Arkansas coaching gig.

28, 2002, to replace Nolan Richardson, Chancellor John White passed out Heath candy bars at the press conference.

Heath forced a laugh at that, but the Michigan native who had only coached in Michigan and Ohio, looked like he had just parachuted into a bad neighborhood upon seeing the raised hands and hearing the "Wooo, Pig Sooies" when athletic director Frank Broyles led the Hog Call.

"I've got a lot to learn," Heath said, wide-eyed.

Later he recalled of the Hog call, "I still remember that day like it was yesterday. I kind of looked, and my wife kind of looked and it was like, 'What is going on?' It was kind of shocking. But after witnessing the Hog Call at football games and then basketball games, we fell in love with it and became a part of it. It's a tradition that will always remain."

Heath actually handled his first Hog call with aplomb compared to a terrified Honolulu bus driver. Nolan Richardson's Razorbacks had just won the 1994 Rainbow Classic in Honolulu when the charter bus full of Hog fans suddenly started calling the Hogs. The bus driver wheeled off the road in the nighttime traffic, turned off the lights and cowered in his seat. It took gentle persuasion that he wasn't about to become a sacrificial victim to some kind of occult rite before the bus rolled again.

Too Old to Outlast Frank

During Heath's introductory press conference, a writer observed the 37-year-old coach had his master's degree in sports administration.

"Are you checking credentials?" Heath asked, bringing down the house in the wake of all the fuss about credentials since George O'Leary had just lost his football coaching job at Notre Dame for a falsely hyped resume.

The reporter persisted.

"No," the reporter said, "I just want to know if you want the athletic director's chair some day."

"He won't live long enough," Broyles, then 77, interrupted.

Broyles has been either Arkansas's head football coach or athletic director since 1958. He did both both jobs from 1973-76 until he retired from coaching and signed on in 2003 for five more years as AD.

Keep Talking

With the once mighty Richardson regime fallen to 14-15 in his last year, and with that team's top scorers either graduating or, in sophomore J.J. Sullinger's case, transferring, and top early signee Andre Igoudala getting a release to switch to Arizona, it was a short end of the stick that Heath had for his 2002-2003 Razorback debut season.

He didn't lose his sense of humor, though.

When the Hogs were about to play Tennessee and its notorious trash talker, Ron Slay, Heath was asked if he fretted Slay's talk would get in his players' heads.

"Everybody else is getting into their heads," Heath said. "Maybe it will help."

Alas, a more mature Slay kept his mouth shut. Slay let his 23 points do the talking in Tennessee's 70-62 triumph at Walton.

Triumphant in Defeat

Heath doesn't kid anybody that the 9-19 record his first team Hog suffered is something to brag about, but the lack of finger-pointing from the players he inherited from

Nolan Richardson and the ones he brought in was something of a marvel.

"We were still cohesive and getting along and trying to work together," Heath said. "I do believe the adversity we worked through that year is going to make us stronger."

The Razorback fans amazed him start to finish both years.

"I'm in awe of the fans how they responded," Heath said. "The Georgia game (a rout by half) was a difficult game. I had traveled that day because of the NCAA investigation and got back just before the game and Georgia got us down 30. We cut it to 12 or 13 and the fan support... that meant a lot to the players and coaches."

Check This Out

Kendrick Davis, one of Heath's two signees for his first Razorback team, was too eager to lend a hand.

"It was the second exhibition game," Heath said. "And I told Kendrick Davis to get in the game. He was so excited he ran right into the game without checking in. I had to yell at him, 'Hold on, Kendrick! You've got to go to the scorer's table.'"

From Baseline to Baseline

Winning at Vanderbilt, with its uniquely configured Memorial Gym where the benches are on opposite baselines, has been tough for even great Hog teams. Yet for this 9-19 outfit of 2002-2003, its lone road victory was at Vandy.

"That was a special game for all of us," Heath said. "Even though I felt like I cheated the University because I only coached half the game. Once they left your end of the court, you were just a spectator like everybody else. The guys handled that situation very well."

Heath got to coach a whole game against the 22nd-ranked Commodores on the conventional Walton Arena floor in 2004.

Arkansas won that, too.

Brewer and the Future

As Ronnie Brewer was named to the SEC All-Freshman team for 2003-2004, coach Stan Heath said how pivotal the guard and son of former Razorback All-American Ron Brewer will be in turning the Razorbacks from 12-16 into the postseason team he projects for 2004-2005.

"How the Razorbacks go, so goes Ronnie Brewer. Trust me on that," Arkansas coach Stan Heath said. "When Ronnie plays well, we are a different team. The games we've won or had success in, Ronnie Brewer has played well. I really feel like he is the key to our future success. With his versatility, he has the ability to lift other players up and really elevate everybody's game."

No Meat on These Bones

Reporting a stringy 6-9 and under 200 pounds, forward Vincent Hunter instantly was presented food by the shovelful when reporting as a Razorback freshman in 2003-2004.

"We were trying to add some weight to Vincent Hunter," Heath said, "and (trainer) Dave England was coordinating the training table. We were having a lot of chicken and wondering why Vincent wasn't eating enough chicken. Vincent said, I know I've got to eat, I just don't like chicken with bones in it. So we had to switch from chicken breasts to nuggets. So he had to have boneless chicken as well as pancakes at every meal. And a couple of others with pancakes, too. We've got finicky guys. Gourmet food wouldn't mean anything to these guys, it's burgers, pancakes, nuggets."

Tickets to Trouble

Coming back from major knee surgery that sidelined him the previous season, senior guard Charles Tatum probably was Arkansas's most popular among the Walton Arena faithful in 2003-2004.

He did lose two fans in one night, though.

"Chuck Tatum had two girls on the ticket list," Heath said, "and they both showed up at the same time to pick up their tickets. He got busted. He's got a different girlfriend now."

Bigger Talent

Signing some hefty big men to go with top returning guards Jonathon "Pookie" Modica, the Smackover native second-team All-SEC in 2003-04, and Ronnie Brewer give his Razorbacks a big chance to be significantly better in 2004-2005 than the 9-19, 12-16, and 14-15 of the immediate three seasons past, Heath believes.

"This is the first season," Arkansas's now third-year coach said, "I feel like we'll be able to play the way I feel like we are capable of playing—at a faster pace and with a more physical team. The emergence of an inside presence is important. We'll be more versatile with better ball skills. I think chemistry is the big thing with this team, because I think there is enough talent to be a postseason team. When's the last time you saw Arkansas play another SEC team and beforehand say, 'You know what? Arkansas has more talent than that other team.' Last year I thought Ole Miss was one of the struggling teams in our league, but we didn't have anybody that could match up with Justin Reed. This is the first time I feel like when we take the floor there will be a portion of games and we can look at the layup lines and think, 'We've got a little more than they've got.'"

Part Three

Baseball

Borys, the Pope and Home Cooking

Borys Malczycki spoke Polish-accented Ebonics with an Arkansas twang. An Arkansas graduate assistant football coach, basketball referee, baseball umpire and later a Pabst Blue Ribbon beer distributor and then a high school principal, Borys grew up in Poland to a family of nobility who lost everything when Russia took over his country. Then Nazi Germany took over Poland when Borys was a boy during World War II. He lived in a Nazi-occupied work camp for a while that was visited by Hitler and then bombed two days later when Allied troops received erroneous information that Hitler was still on the premises.

Borys was still a schoolboy when his family emigrated, thanks to a Catholic Relief Fund, to Little Rock where he grew up playing any sport with a ball among blacks and poor whites.

Borys became as American as apple pie but never forgot the Old Country.

No sooner had smoke from the Vatican signaled Poland's John Paul being named Pope than Borys burst through the Broyles Complex shouting, "The Pope's a home boy! The Pope's a home boy!"

Home Cooking

As a Southwest Conference umpire during Arkansas's SWC baseball days, Borys was naturally regarded with suspicion by coaches visiting Fayetteville.

So the first time that Borys called a borderline pitch, a strike against a Baylor hitter, Baylor Coach Mickey Sullivan snapped, "That's home cooking."

"That's not home cooking," Borys retorted.

The next pitch bounced.

"Strike!" Borys bellowed, wheeling towards the Baylor dugout. "Now that's home cooking!"

Sullivan surrendered.

"Go back to calling them the way you were," Sullivan sighed.

Snow Job

A blizzard prevented the regular SWC officiating crew from working a SWC basketball game in Fayetteville during the Eddie Sutton era.

Borys was one of the usual suspects rounded up locally as replacement refs.

"Oh, boy, Borys!" Razorback center Joe Kleine shouted when the officials came out before tipoff. "Six on five!"

Hey, Ump, Who's 'We'?

Between games of a baseball doubleheader Borys umped between Norm DeBriyn's Razorbacks and Southern Illinois, Borys used the press box phone to call his wife and say he was running late.

"We lost the first game," Borys said.

"We!" SIU's radio announcer gasped. "The umpire says we?"

He needn't have worried. SIU won the second game, too, without any interference from Borys.

Though he obviously loved the Hogs, Borys actually was a pretty good and impartial official.

DeBriyn, virtually an uncle to Borys's three children, even got tossed a couple of times by Borys during games.

The Bud Man Toasts Borys

Perhaps the best tribute to Borys, who died in 1998, came from a rival beer distributor. Way before Borys died, Bob McBride, the Budweiser distributor in Fayetteville, was overheard offering to buy a man a beer.

"Appreciate the offer," the man said, "But I'll be buying myself a Pabst. I've known Borys a long time."

"No problem," McBride, smiling, said, deftly buying the man a Pabst, "I like that rascal, too."

Everybody did, it seems.

A Dr. Kevorkian Ahead of His Time

The late Ed Froning was one of Fayetteville's radio pioneers and certainly the pioneer of what has long been the Razorback baseball radio network. Like most everybody who knows him, Ed loved Norm DeBriyn and put so much time into setting up broadcasting the baseball coach's games that it's a wonder he made any profit off them.

But he no doubt did. The station manager at the long-since sold Fayetteville radio station KNWA, Ed could be officious and demanding, but he was always right.

Like the time I was doing the play by play with Ed doing the color on one of those Razorback versus some hapless NAIA directional school games the Razorbacks played over spring break.

As I was describing the Razorbacks' 14th run of the second inning, Ed pulled the plug.

"This is a mismatch," Ed interrupted. "No contest here. No contest. That's it. We're going back to the studio."

Too Much Spice in the Vinegar

As a station manager, Ed was old school with a radio station that played old songs. None of the blue language coloring today's airwaves was going to cross his station. Except maybe once.

It was between games of a doubleheader, and Arkansas had just been upset by one of those directional schools the Hogs were used to plundering.

Pitching coach Tom Hilton, graciously filling time with us in the interim, observed, "We just looked like we were going through the motions. We've got to come out there with some piss and vinegar this game."

Ed's headset about dislodged for his exploding veins.

"Piss and vinegar?!!!" he gasped during the commercial break. "Piss and vinegar?!!! We can't have that on the air! Can't have it! Can't have it! Can't have it!"

He was well into his umpteenth "Can't have it" when the commercial break ended, and we were back on the air.

Partners, Bah, Humbug!!!

Ed was free with advice, and Norm took it freely, except once. Somebody with a business deal had offered to cut Norm in with a partnership. What did Ed think?

"Partnership?!!!" Ed exploded in vintage piss and vinegar reaction. "Partnership?!! No one should go into partnership on anything except marriage. And I'm not even sure about that!!!"

Norm remembers it well, and ruefully.

"I should have listened to Ed," Norm said. "Because I went in on the deal and lost my butt. Ed was always right."

Norm's Laundered Money

Retired Razorback business manager Ray Shipman always described retired baseball coach Norm DeBriyn as "honest as the day is long." However, Shipman did know that Norm was involved in "laundered money. DeBriyn's Razorbacks were hosting SMU, and SMU had the worst baseball program in the Southwest Conference. It had been raining solidly all week and had turned the basepaths at George Cole Field into a swamp.

"Norm wasn't about to let SMU get away without playing them," Shipman said. "So he got a bunch of old tires and set fire to them to dry up the basepaths."

"It worked to the point that the series was played and Arkansas won, but not without paying for it.

"SMU came in wearing the whitest of uniforms," Shipman said. "But after sliding on all that carbon they were coal black. We had to buy SMU new uniforms."

SMU must have sold them for a profit. Shortly thereafter, the Mustangs gave up their baseball program.

Green, Green Grass of Home

Lettering as a Razorback second baseman in the 1970s, Ralph Bradbury remembers coach Norm DeBriyn coming to grips with the marijuana issue of the times.

Norm gathered the troops for a dugout lecture.

"He said to the group," Bradbury recalled, 'You know ... you know ... when it comes to marijuana, as far as I am concerned, it's all cut and dried.'"

An eternity passed of smothered smirks.

"We all put our heads down and started chuckling," Bradbury said. "And then he figured out what he said, and yelled 'Get your ass out there!,' and made us run."

Coach Norm DeBriyn's thoughts on marijuana gave his players a good laugh: "As far as I'm concerned, it's all cut and dried." DeBriyn quickly figured out the joke was on him, and his players' laughter turned into laps.

Turning a Deaf Ear

Larry Wallace was deaf, but that didn't prevent him from being the regular second baseman on Arkansas's 1979 national runnerup team. DeBriyn always treated Wallace as a regular infielder, even when he was apprenticing as a young reserve behind Ralph Bradbury.

"Larry was deaf and was working with me at second," Bradbury said, "and he throws the ball the wrong way on the infield deal we're doing. Coach started yelling, 'Wallace! Wallace!' And I said, 'Coach, he just won't listen, will he?'"

A Bit of England

Former Razorback pitcher Pat Anderson's use of trainer David England's name provided some British humor that coach Norm DeBriyn didn't appreciate.

"Someone got hit with a batting practice pitch and went down hurt," Anderson recalled. "And Norm goes, 'Where the hell is England?'

"And I hollered back, 'It's across the ocean!' He started running at me."

Pagnozzi Converts to Arkie Catcher

Tom Pagnozzi transferred out of an Arizona junior college to Arkansas in 1983 specifically to convert from third base to catcher under coach Norm DeBriyn as a ticket to the big leagues.

The ticket became round trip. After catching in the bigs a dozen years for the St. Louis Cardinals, Pagnozzi now is back at

Arkansas as an assistant under another DeBriyn protégé, Razorback coach Dave Van Horn, after catching in the bigs a dozen years for the St. Louis Cardinals.

"Five scouts recommended I learn to be a catcher," Pagnozzi said, "because I didn't hit with enough power to be a Major League third baseman. They said, 'You swing the bat well enough if you learn to catch.'"

He had hit well as a junior college third baseman for many schools to offer him the chance to catch.

"Other schools said, 'You can catch, and if it doesn't work out, you can be our starting third baseman,'" Pagnozzi said. "Norm, I don't know if he was that much smarter or that much dumber, but he looked me in the eye and said, 'You know what? You can come here as a catcher and if it doesn't work out, you may not play, because we've got to recruit a third baseman right now.' That gave me the assuring feeling that he's going to try and make it work, not just move me back to third, which I thought other schools would do."

Though he's lefthanded and never was a catcher, DeBriyn had turned out All-SWC catchers Jeff Hemm and Ronn Reynolds. Reynolds also was an All-American and longtime Major Leaguer catcher, before DeBriyn molded Pagnozzi into the man who would become the St. Louis Cardinals' All-Star catcher throughout the late 1980s and early '90s.

So what's Norm know to be an expert on the position he never played?

"I'm not sure he knows a lot," Pagnozzi said, laughing, "or just thinks he knows a lot. No, he knows. One thing about Norm is he constantly learns. That's why he's been very successful. He stays current and sees drills that work. When he would come up to watch me play in St. Louis he would always watch our drills and ask questions. He and Whitey (Herzog, the former Cardinals' manager) were good friends. Whitey would come down here in the fall to hunt and watch a football game."

Not an Overnight Star

Pagnozzi earned All-Southwest Conference honors his lone Razorback season, but it wasn't an overnight process.

"I got more attention than any player on the club that year because I was learning to catch," Pagnozzi said. "We spent a good 45 minutes a day, basically just him and I on individual drills, blocking drills, catching and throwing. He could have easily put me back there for a couple of games, but said, 'The kid can't catch. We're going to move him to third.' We had Ron Slembarski who was a better defensive catcher but couldn't hit. It would have been easy to play him behind the plate and me at third. But he stuck with Mark Berry at third and me behind the plate and stuck with it. If he hadn't stuck with it, we wouldn't be doing this interview here."

The Third to Catcher Express

Ironically, DeBriyn moved Berry from third to catcher after Pagnozzi signed with St. Louis and later would move outfielder-third baseman Jimmy Kremers behind the plate.

"It worked," Pagnozzi said. "So every year he'd take his third baseman and put him over there, and it worked."

Berry, the bullpen coach with Cincinnati, made it to Triple A as a catcher. Kremers went all the way to the bigs, catching with Atlanta and Montreal.

Giving Back

As for Pagnozzi, he not only earned All-Southwest Conference and became one of the best and most durable

Catcher Tom Pagnozzi transferred from junior college to Arkansas, from third base to catcher, from Arkansas to the Big Leagues, and finally from the big leagues back to Arkansas, where he now sits on the bench alongside Hogs head coach Dave Van Horn.

catchers in the Cardinals' history, he was inducted into the University of Arkansas Sports Hall of Honor, and has become a philanthropist, with his Pagnozzi Charities centering most of its good works in Northwest Arkansas.

Pretty amazing for a guy who lived here just one year in college.

DeBriyn fosters an urge to give back.

It was former Razorbacks Tim Lollar, Johnny Ray and Kevin McReynolds who became big Major League stars, but not so big that they didn't remember their roots. They and their agent, Little Rock-born Tom Selakovich, donated the money that lit the old George Cole Field in 1985.

"We wanted to do it for the university," McReynolds said. "But we did it for Coach DeBriyn."

Selakovich minced no words.

"We would have never put up the money," Selakovich said, "for those lights if it wasn't for Coach DeBriyn. $37,500 was a lot of money back then, but Coach DeBriyn was such a tremendous man that we decided we all were going to do this for him. He meant so much to us as a man."

All were saddened somewhat when DeBriyn announced after the 2002 season that his 33rd year at the Hog helm was his last. But all were so happy that Norm finished with a flourish, with his underdog Hogs going all the way to the rubber game of the NCAA Super Regional at nationally second-seeded Clemson. What pleased them most is that Norm chose to retire instead of it being chosen for him.

"I'm glad he's retiring on his terms," Lollar said from Lakeview, Colorado where the All-America letfy pitcher-DH is now a lefthanded-teaching golf pro. "Just a class guy. He was a huge influence on all of us and made Arkansas a recognized place to go."

Thrown Out by the Book

An umpire once threw the book at recently retired Razorback coach Norm DeBriyn before DeBriyn could read the book to him. DeBriyn recounted the tale during the Razorbacks' annual baseball reunion in 2004.

"Wichita State's pitcher was using a sleeve of contrasting colors," DeBriyn said. "I knew you couldn't do that, and we were getting our ass beat, and I was going to make them change because Texas did that to us one time. So I went out there and said, 'Make him change.' And the umpire said, 'Let's just play baseball.' And I said, 'But ...' and he said, 'Let's go play baseball.' So I went back to the dugout, got the rule book, and we found the rule and I was excited. I put that sucker to the right page, put it in my back pocket and went back out there and said,

'Make him take that white undersleeve off. I've got it right here in the rule book!'

"He says, 'Don't get that rule book out here! Don't show me up!' That's when I lost it. I reached back for the rule book and I couldn't get it out. And he tossed me and all the while I was arguing while trying to get the rule book out of my pocket."

The Hogs were too amused to assist their arguing coach.

"We were dying laughing," first baseman Nick Pitts said. "He was arguing while jerking his pants up and couldn't get the rule book out."

Pat Anderson, who pitched for DeBriyn's Hogs in 1977 and '78 and umpired some Razorback games in the 1980s before moving to Pine Bluff, laughed at DeBriyn recounting the rule book story.

"At least you didn't have the rule out book out when I ran your butt," Anderson said.

Anderson recalled tossing his old coach after voiding a Razorback home run.

"Mike Loggins hit a home run," Anderson said, "and crossed the runner at first base because the runner went halfway, waiting to see if it had been caught or gone out and didn't see Loggins. Marty Pattin, the Kansas coach saw it.

"Norm comes out saying, 'He didn't pass him.' I believe Dave Van Horn (the Hogs' head coach since 2003 and a former DeBriyn assistant) was coaching first base and he didn't have a problem. But Norm comes out screaming. Then he says I bumped him, and I said he bumped me, and I said, 'Just get out! Just get out of here!'"

Better a Short Stop than a Long Talk

Rob Kauffman, the Razorbacks' shortstop of 1978, who became third baseman in 1979 and most of '80, still hadn't cleared the cobwebs from an unauthorized night on the town in

Austin where Norm DeBriyn's Razorbacks were early arrivals for the 1980 Southwest Conference Tournament.

His hotel room phone rang. Chillingly.

"Norm calls me up," Kauffman recalled at the 2002 Razorback baseball reunion, "and says, 'Hey, Robby, we need to talk about a few things.' I thought, 'I'm in deep water because of some things that had gone down the night before.' I was thinking, 'I've got to come up with something pretty quick. Not necessarily lie, but buy me some time.' And when he came out with a move to another position, shortstop because Todd Zacher had gotten hurt, I said, 'You bet! I'm ready! Are we done? Can I get out of here?'"

Kauffman escaped unscathed but not necessarily undetected.

"Years had gone by," Kauffman recalled, "And Norm said, 'You know, you were really excited about going back to short-stop.'

"I said, 'I was, Coach. But in actuality, I thought I was getting called on the carpet for something else.'

"He said, 'You probably could have.'

"And I said, 'Probably so.'"

DeBriyn didn't want Kauffman squirming too much to excel.

And excel Rob did.

"I had a good SWC Tournament," Kauffman recalled, "and then we beat ORU, 2-1 in the first round at Regionals. Pole (first baseman John Hennell) and (Kevin) McReynolds went deep, and those were the only hits we had. (All-America pitcher Steve) Krueger got in a little hole in the ninth and I made a play to help get us out of it."

The '79 team stunned the college baseball world by not only winning the Regional at Tallahassee, Florida after a third-place Southwest Conference finish, but at the College World Series finished second in the country losing 2-1 in the championship game to California State-Fullerton.

"We didn't have a bunch of stars in '79," Kauffman said. "When I first got here in '77 we had (All-SWC pitcher/All-

American DH Tim Lollar. He was the big duck on the pond, which was justified. But '79, we were tight because of no-names who had been through so much and thought, 'We had a chance to do something.'"

Early Norm

Richard Miller, now a longtime attorney in Fayetteville, came out of Texarkana to letter as a starting pitcher for DeBriyn's Razorbacks from 1972-74. That encompassed Arkansas's last two years as a vagabond baseball independent, with the '73 team surprising by qualifying for NCAA Regionals, and the Hogs' maiden SWC season in 1974.

All Arkansas's home games were at Legion Field and American Legion park, way off campus. Not only was Norm's ballpark substandard, but the lack of funding had him settling for pitching coaches virtually working for free while they completed graduate school projects.

"We had one guy who was all theory," Miller said. "I don't think he ever had played in a baseball game in his life. I'd make a routine play, and the pitching coach would yell, 'Richard Miller, that's the greatest play I've seen in my life!' And you would hear that from the dugout and I would cringe and say to myself, 'Don't be telling me that.'"

DeBriyn, though, was an unrelenting critic if the team gave anything less than its best.

"When I was a freshman," Miller recalled, "Gerald Hannahs (later to pitch for the Montreal Expos) was pitching and didn't warm up enough and we ended up losing a game to a little, old Oklahoma school. That's not supposed to happen. We were on the road, but Norm ran us in the outfield after the game was over. He let you come in and go to the bus according to how you had done in the game. Finally at the end, Hannahs is running, running and running by himself. And finally Norm gets us all the on bus and Norm is screaming and yelling at us how we are a bunch of prima donnas and everything, and he loses his voice. He's trying to yell and he's just standing there with his lips moving and nothing coming out. Finally he gave up and just sat down. It was only because he lost his voice and couldn't yell anymore."

John Jenkins on the Ball

John Jenkins made quite a name for himself as an innovator of the run-and-shoot offense when he was first the University of Houston's offensive coordinator and then the Cougars' head football coach.

But as a collegian he was at Arkansas playing fullback in football and first base and DH in baseball. He was an avid weightlifter and as a baseball player in the on-deck circle and between pitches he always seemed to be flexing in short sleeves to impress any fair damsels attending the game.

One time, Miller recalls, Jenkins outdid himself.

"Jenkins gets hit with a baseball in the head and he goes down," Miller said. "The fans, the few that are there, go Oooh! Jenkins hops up, dusts himself off, picks up the ball, flips it to the umpire and says, 'You had better check that ball and see if it's OK.' And then he trots to first.'"

Mind Boggling

Probably the greatest single play in Razorback history was a double play scored 5-3-2 in your scorebook only the 2, catcher Doyle Wilson, made the putout covering third base.

The throw from first baseman Dave Patterson and Wilson's tag was the final out in the 1985 Regional victory over

Florida State in Tallahassee, Florida that propelled DeBriyn's Razorbacks into the College World Series.

While others celebrated, DeBriyn recalled, relief pitcher Tim Deitz stood, blinking in shock.

"It was a high chopper that went over my head," Deitz recalled, noting there was one out and a runner at first. "I was going back for it, the shortstop was coming in for it and (third baseman Jeff) King caught it behind me and threw it to first. The runner rounded second and saw nobody was covering third, and Doyle headed down there. Patterson led him like a quarterback throwing to a receiver.

"It went from being what I thought would be a base hit into a double play."

A picture in the Tallahassee paper the next day showed Wilson shouting and applying the tag simultaneously and also showed second baseman Keith Kerns pursuing the runner in case the throw went awry.

"I still say the '85 team was the best team they had here," Ellis Roby, the '85 team's regular second baseman, said. "To not lose a game in May and be 51-15 overall, that was a team. We had eight guys drafted off that team. And they were successful off the field."

Underarm Alarm

Tim Deitz came to Arkansas out of the Tulsa area as one of the Razorbacks' most highly recruited pitchers but looked done after continued arm problems led to reconstructive surgery.

"I had the surgery," Deitz said, "and was just shagging balls in the outfield. Norm and (pitching coach) Dave Jorn (now also the pitching coach under Dave Van Horn) had talked about it together at dinner, about throwing sidearm in relief. I tried it, and it felt fine. But I said, 'The proof will be how much it hurts tomorrow,' but it didn't. I threw a couple of pitches and it felt okay. And I pitched in a couple of games over spring break and then went down to Houston for a conference series and saved a game there. It was all fastballs. And Coach Jorn was my pitching coach in Liberal, Kansas that summer and we worked on a slider."

Deitz became a sidearm star exceeded when Phillip Stidham jumped from jack of all trades and master of none to be the ace reliever who pitched Arkansas into the 1989 College World Series and led the 1990 Hogs to their only SWC regular-season championship.

"Phillip Stidham came on doing that," Deitz said, "and had like a 1.07 ERA. He got in the big leagues (with Detroit) but when he did, they had him throwing over the top. What was amazing is he came over here as a shortstop."

A Night to Remember

If Ralph Kraus ever forgets lighting up George Cole Field after it was already lit, some Razorback fan somewhere will remind him, even way out in Seattle where he now lives.

Kraus's ninth-inning home run beat Texas in the first Southwest Conference game in 1985 under the lights donated to George Cole Field by former Razorbacks and major league stars Tim Lollar, Johnny Ray and Kevin McReynolds and their agent, Tom Selakovich.

"I came into the game as a pinch hitter earlier for Steve Clements," Kraus recalled. "I hit the ball hard the first time up. I remember a friend of mine who played for Texas talked about (Texas pitcher) Curt Krippner and how hard he threw the ball. I was just trying to get a hit with Norm Roberts on second. And when I did hit it, I thought, 'Wow! It might go out!' I was just trying to get a hit and then it became a big deal. And to this day it's still a big deal. Every time I come to Arkansas, somebody always brings it up. And then the next day, Tim Deitz, my roommate, closes out a 2-1 victory."

A Two-Degree Man

Kraus, one of the rare, four-year major college baseball players since so many either come as junior college transfers or sign professionally after they are draft eligible following their junior year, has two degrees. One is from Arkansas and one is from Texas.

"When we went to Austin my senior year," Kraus recalled, "they couldn't believe I was still around. They actually gave me a graduation gift. You remember that Wild Bunch (a rowdy, witty group of Longhorn baseball fans). The attorney general of Texas was actually a part of that. They gave me a diploma that said, 'Would you please graduate and get out of here?' They didn't like us much. And we didn't like them, either. But it was fun to play them."

A Frenchman in Left Field

Crossett's Mike Loggins earned All-America honors as a center fielder for the 1985 Razorbacks, but he recalled being thrown to the wolves as a freshman left fielder when balls caromed off the George Cole Stadium wall like it was a racquetball court.

"Playing that wall is like being sent to France," Loggins said. "And the only French you know is 'Oui, oui.'"

Supreme Guilt

A current Arkansas Supreme Court Justice once judged himself harshly when he played Razorback baseball.

Tom Glaze played for the baseball Hogs in the days when then-assistant basketball coach—later to become head basketball coach P.T. "Duddy" Waller—and football trainer Bill "Ground Hog" Ferrell coached the baseball team.

"Both Duddy and Bill Ferrell were old school," Glaze, an Arkansas Supreme Court Justice, said. "When you stole second you were told to go in hard and take out the infielder. I never felt so bad in my life as when I went hard into home and I hit a catcher and broke his ankle. You weren't trying to do that. But you were supposed to separate the ball from the catcher."

Take the Bus

G laze said he played on the team that became the vehicle for the Razorbacks to travel by bus instead of caravans for road games.

"We had gone on a Southern tour and played Mississippi State and Southern Mississippi," Glaze said. "And we were coming back in cars. We were passing on an incline one night on a Mississippi highway and we got in the wrong lane. We saw these headlights coming. It pulled us both off the shoulder. That was the last time we used cars. That was one legacy we left to later teams was to have a bus."

Alworth's Worth

L ance Alworth not only was a Razorback football great who made the NFL Hall of Fame as a San Diego Chargers' wide receiver, but he was one of the greatest all-round athletes the UA produced.

Baseball, track, Alworth could do it all.

All that was fine with Frank Broyles to help entice Alworth to Arkansas. But like most football coaches, Broyles cringed at the thought of one of his stars getting hurt in another sport even if it was the football trainer, Ground Hog Ferrell, doing the coaching.

"I remember the time Lance ran into the wooden fence at Fairgrounds Park," Glaze said. "Frank yelled from the stands, 'That boy gets hurt, you are in big trouble, Ground Hog!' It was obvious Broyles's main interest was football."

Luckily, Glaze said, it was Alworth's, too.

"Lance Alworth could hit the ball a mile," Glaze said, "but he couldn't hit a curve ball. He picked football, and it was the right place."

Broyles, apprised some 42 years later of Glaze recalling him admonishing Ground Hog about Alworth, said, "I'm sure I did say that. Lance was such a great athlete. He could have a great spring football practice in the morning, help the baseball team win, and then run over to the track and run a 9.6 100 for the track team. And he could throw, kick, run. He could do anything."

Taking a Chance

T hough physically the most gifted player to play for DeBriyn, Arkansas native Kevin McReynolds still figured it was a gamble for Norm to sign him in 1979.

Kevin McReynolds was appreciative that Coach DeBriyn took a gamble on a kid from Arkansas. It gave McReynolds the chance to attend Coach's School of Hard Knocks.

"He took a chance on me," McReynolds said, "and I like to think I made him look kinda good, too."

Mac always could cover a lot of ground with a little sentence as easy as he covered ground in the outfield without ever looking rushed.

"He really did take a chance on me, though," McReynolds continued. "There just weren't that many Arkansas kids. But me and Tabor (Little Rock native Scott Tabor still leads Arkansas with 34 wins) came the same year. He taught everybody that a little hard work never hurt anybody. Only for him it wasn't just a little hard work. He'd work hard from sunup long into the night."

School of Hard Knocks

DeBriyn not only coached from the school of hard knocks, he personified it, McReynolds recalled, laughing.

He recalled DeBriyn at the 1979 Southwest Conference Tournament in Austin.

"I remember he's coaching third," McReynolds mused, "and (Arkansas first baseman John) Hennell, who is left handed smoked one the other way. It got Norm right on the knee and he wouldn't touch it. Those Texas fans were just waiting for him to rub it so they could get on him, but he never did. And we rallied a little that inning so he was out there awhile. I mean he had to be in pain. When he got to the dugout, that knee was huge."

Chesty Makes the Call

Back in the early 1970s when the Hogs played on an American Legion field, they often had an old American Legion umpire, Paul "Chesty" Foster, umping their games.

Chesty was pretty past his prime and kind of hard of hearing, which made his calls all the louder. Norm was coaching third when a runner got thrown out at the close of a bizarre, convoluted play that had Chesty running all over the field. While making the call, Chesty raced in, arms pinwheeling and yelling, "Out! Out! Out" dramatically, and perhaps prematurely. Norm jumped to argue but ceased. You can't argue when you are convulsed laughing.

Upon his third shout of "Out!," Chesty hit the pileup of the sliding runner and third baseman. He tripped over them both and did his own slide at Norm's feet.

Another Nolo Contendre

Norm had another third-base argument never lodged, though the rule book seemed on his side. Baylor coach Mickey Sullivan was coaching third when he did more than just signal his advancing runner to hold up at third. Sullivan made contact with the runner. Interference, apparently.

Only trouble was, Norm would have had to step over doctors and trainers to argue with the umpires. The Baylor runner plowed into Sullivan and knocked him cold.

Norm was just too decent to argue while one of his coaching pals was toted out on a stretcher.

Norm vs. Gomer

Longtime Razorback broadcasters Mike Nail and Chuck Barrett told of a Razorback baseball bus ride to Oxford, Mississippi during which coach Norm DeBriyn and the driver, Gene "Gomer" Estep, got into a heated argument about an old tractor they had just passed in a yard.

"The grass was so tall you could barely see the tractor," Nail said. "And I bet the tractor hadn't run in 30 years. But Norm says something like, 'That's a John Deere Model XFB' and Gomer says something like, 'No! That's a Model ZDF.'

"And they start arguing like the other one is an idiot. Pretty soon you hear, 'Oh, yeah, well, $20 says it is.'

"So Gomer wheels across the median," Barrett said, "and we drive back. Jay Eddings (then the pitching coach) gets out and has to climb over a fence to get to the tractor and check it out. Turns out Norm was right. Gomer goes to pay him, and Norm won't take it until Gomer yells, 'Take your *^$# money,' and throws it at him."

Gomer's anger didn't last. He drove DeBriyn's teams for decades.

Learning Too Late

On the last pre-Southwest Conference Tournament baseball trip from Fayetteville to play Oral Roberts University in Tulsa, coach Norm DeBriyn got in to drive one of the team vans out of the Broyles Complex driveway and realized he had forgotten something in his office.

"Damn!" DeBriyn said.

As players nudged each other and nodded, DeBriyn bustled out of the van to his office, came back with what he had forgotten but without his briefcase.

"Damn!"

Another trip to the office.

Tim Clancy, a bemused fifth-year senior, watched DeBriyn get reseated, and reach into his pocket for the van keys.

Wrong keys.

"Aw, geez," DeBriyn ranted. "I don't know anything."

Clancy sighed.

"Now he tells me," the senior said.

Easy Ed

E asy Ed Wallace won the Southwest Conference batting championship as a designated hitter but had a nightmare Southwest Conference Tournament, which Texas hosted in Austin.

The Longhorns' fabled group of fans, called "The Wild Bunch," unmercifully rode the stocky DH who was built somewhat like two men sitting down. "Whoosh! Whoosh! Whoosh!" they whooshed with each pitch that Ed flailed forlornly at as the Hogs lost to Texas and fell into the loser's bracket.

DeBriyn didn't start him when the Hogs climbed back to get another chance at Texas in the tournament finals. With the Hogs down by a lot late but with men on, DeBriyn glanced over at Ed. Was he still too frazzled to pinch hit?

Easy Ed grabbed a bat, and while still in the dugout smiled and said, "Want to hear a roar?"

He indeed got the roar and then some.

"Whoosh! Whoosh! Whoo…"

Wallace knocked the sh out of "Whoosh." Easy Ed hit that third pitch so hard he netted the first and only triple of his collegiate career.

Arkansas still lost the game and the SWC Tournament, but Easy Ed won his war and later would help eliminate Texas from the '79 College World Series.

Rain Man

G ary Murphy was pitcher from Pennsylvania for DeBriyn's Razorbacks who talked liked Tony Danza or Marlon Brando's famed character in *On the Waterfront*.

"I coulda been a contender," would have been a perfect line for Murphy.

Two innings before a cloudburst washed out the game, Murphy got tagged for a towering home run by Oklahoma State slugger Pete Incaviglia.

"I tink dat's what brought da rain," Murphy told the media.

That's the Way the Ball Bounces

Incaviglia, who later played with the Philadelphia Phillies, set a collegiate record of 47 home runs in a season. However, as an outfielder, it's a wonder he didn't match the 47 homers with 47 errors.

The left field corner at Arkansas's old George Cole Field (now Lady Razorback Yard for softball) was tricky to play, even for Razorback left fielders playing it every day. For Incaviglia, on a day the Hogs were hitting it hard, it meant repeatedly passing the caroms like ships in the night.

"You all got a regular pinball machine out here," Incaviglia told former *Arkansas Gazette* stringer David Dickinson.

Life in the Pitts

Two great Razorback coaches happily admit to having second thoughts about Nick Pitts, a walk-on from Mountain Home who persevered four years, including a redshirt year, for Norm DeBriyn and then as a senior for Dave Van Horn.

DeBriyn saw a work ethic and nothing else and continually advised Pitts to transfer to a smaller school. Pitts doggedly stuck with it, and DeBriyn stuck with Pitts, making him his first baseman for the 2002 team that went to the NCAA Regionals.

With University of Miami first baseman Haas Pratt transferring to Arkansas in 2003, Van Horn figured Pitts would waste his time staying on, even if he had been a starter the year before.

Pitts didn't play much first base in 2003, but he ended up playing nearly every game either in left field or third base.

After the season, Van Horn called Pitts "my favorite player."

Pitts's senior-year work ethic was contagious and helped set the tone for Van Horn's 2004 team winning the SEC.

"It wasn't encouraging," Pitts said of his initial reviews from DeBriyn and Van Horn. "Maybe they just know how to spark somebody. They told me the exact same thing at the beginning, that you are probably not going to play here, and at the end they both said, 'Thank you for working hard.'"

Can he compare the two coaches?

"They both are two completely different coaches," Pitts said. "But they have this in common, they are hard-nosed and want to win. Obviously Coach D proved he could win, one of the best coaches in history. And I think Van Horn will follow in his footsteps."

Fatherly Advice from Pops

None of DeBriyn's great players showed any more consistency both as a Razorback and a major leaguer than Johnny Ray, the Razorbacks' second baseman in 1978 and '79, and an All-Star with the Pittsburgh Pirates and California Angels.

None knew the game better or had any better makeup to be a major league manager or coach, yet Ray immediately ended his baseball time and came back year round to his Choteau, Oklahoma home with the close of his playing days.

Ray did so, he said, largely on Hall of Fame advice from the late Willie Stargell, called "Pops" because of his father-figure influence on the Pirates as a veteran first baseman and later as a coach.

Fans can thank Razorback 2B Johnny Ray—arguably the best player to ever play Arkansas baseball—for the gift of light at Baum Stadium.

"It goes back to something Willie Stargell told me," Ray said. "That he put 20-something years into the game, and his son grew up without him being around. He said, 'Johnny, if you have one thing to do in your life, it's to be more of a father.' That's why I thought about it that when my playing days were over, I wouldn't be in baseball."

Ray continues to be in Razorback baseball. The stadium lights that he and fellow Razorbacks Tim Lollar and Kevin McReynolds and their agent, Tom Selakovich, donated to George Cole Field still light the way for Baum Stadium.

The donation was considerable.

"It all goes back to enjoying your experience here," Ray said of making such a gift just a few years into his Major League career, "and Coach DeBriyn and everybody. So being able to give something back is what that's all about. Coach DeBriyn is more than a baseball coach. Everybody who knows him feels that same way. When you are around people like that, you want to do something for them. I know that thanks to him I had the springboard to play professionally."

Lucky No-Talents

Of the four Norm DeBriyn-coached teams that went to the College World Series, none came from more overachieving, humble origins than the 1987 team.

"Jeff King, Ralph Kraus and Dave Patterson were our three star players in '86," Troy Eklund, an outfielder on the '87 team, recalled, "and we lost them all. In the fall, Seminole Junior College came in and played a tripleheader against us and won them all. Our coaches were telling us, 'You are not any good.' But in the spring the Southwest Conference started and we kept winning and kept winning, and still the coaches didn't say we were any good. 'You guys are just lucky.' We got to a Regional and beat Auburn and finally they told us, 'You are a halfway-decent team.' But the whole year they had been telling us we were lousy because I guess they thought if we didn't think we had talent, we would keep on playing hard."

Tools of Ignorance

Since baseball's advent, catching gear has been called "the tools of ignorance."

Nobody donned the tools of ignorance feeling any more ignorant than outfielder Jimmy Kremers in his emergency catching debut for Norm DeBriyn's Hogs against Oral Roberts.

"We were behind in the game," Kremers said, "and we started pinch hitting and pinch running to come back, and we used up our catchers and we come back, and all of a sudden it's 'Who is going to catch?' And Coach DeBriyn says, 'Kremers, you are catching!' I was scared to death. Coach DeBriyn had talked to me about catching, but I hadn't caught an inning. So I get back there and Ray Harris is pitching and everything went OK. The game ended with me somehow catching a pop fly."

It was the start of what became a Major League career, catching for the Braves and Expos.

"If I didn't catch," Kremers said, "I never would have made it."

What was DeBriyn's knack for taking players like Tom Pagnozzi and Kremers, who had never caught before, and converting them into major league catchers?

"He's a real student of the game," Kremers said. "What he taught was the same that I was taught at every level. I think there was one advantage for him in getting someone who had never caught because, there are no bad habits to break because he's never done it before."

Basebrawl

The Razorbacks never had a bigger brawl than in the mid-1980s against Oral Roberts in Tulsa. Police had to be summoned, and the game ceased because of the all-over-the-field brawling ensuing from ORU batter Mike Batesole heaving the bat and charging the mound for fisticuffs with Razorback pitcher Kevin Campbell.

"Mike Shambaugh was the hitter before him," Campbell said, "and I had hit him twice. The previous at-bat I just nicked him on the knee. He looked at Batesole and Batesole looked at him and it was, 'Go get him.' Batesole threw the bat while I was delivering the pitch. It got crazy after that. Fans on the field, police getting called. It was crazy. Funny thing is I ended up playing with that guy (Batesole) at Vero Beach. And we laughed about it then."

A pitcher on Arkansas's, 1985 College World Series team, Campbell got drafted after his junior year in '86 and went on to the bigs, pitching for both the Minnesota Twins and Oakland A's.

Instant Success

In 2004, just his second year as Arkansas's head baseball coach, former Razorback second baseman and assistant coach Dave Van Horn took the Razorbacks to the SEC West title, an SEC Overall co-championship with East champion Georgia.

That was just for starters for the former Razorback second baseman and assistant coach summoned from his head coaching position at the University of Nebraska to replace his old coach, retiring Arkansas legend Norm DeBriyn.

After winning the SEC co-championship, Van Horn's Hogs won a NCAA Regional championship at Baum Stadium, clawing out of the loser's bracket to beat Wichita State twice on

Dave Van Horn didn't waste any time after taking over coaching duties for the Hogs. His 2004 squad advanced all the way to the College World Series.

Sunday and finally a Super Regional two-game sweep of Florida State before crowds that for the first time exceeded 10,000 at Baum and advanced to the College World Series, the eight-team tournament determining the national champion at Rosenblatt Stadium in Omaha.

The sizzle turned to fizzle in Omaha with 13-2 and 7-2 losses to Texas and Arizona, but who can complain?

In preseason, this 2004 Hog team that ultimately went 45-24 with four championships, was picked last in the six-team West and 11th overall in the 12-team league by the league coaches in their preseason poll.

"If you had told me before the year," Van Horn said after the Hogs immediately were eliminated by Arizona in Omaha, "we could win 45 games and go to Omaha and lose two, I would take it in a second. I told them to hold their heads up high. We may have gotten more out of a team than anybody in the country. Next year, hopefully, we will be better and also the year after that."

To What Do You Attribute ...?

The stunning success Arkansas achieved didn't prepare Van Horn for a stunning College World Series question from an Atlanta reporter right after the Arizona loss.

Van Horn had coached Nebraska, a school that never had been to the CWS and hasn't since he left, to two CWS appearances that ended with the underdog Cornhuskers falling two games and out.

"You are 0-6 in this tournament as a coach," the reporter stated. "To what do you attribute that?"

Van Horn was dumbfounded.

"Pardon me?" Van Horn replied.

The question was repeated.

"The other team outscored us six times," Van Horn bristled. "You ask a dumb question, you get a dumb answer."

Later, Van Horn confessed, "I should have handled that better and been Mr. Nice Guy. Answering like that just played into his hands."

Maybe, but you can't blame a coach for thinking no good deed goes unpunished going 0-6 at the CWS with three underdog teams when many a good coach from many a good program has never even made it to Omaha.

Casey at the 'Blatt

From Omaha in 2004, there was little joy in Hogville, save maybe Casey at the 'Blatt. Joy would be a stretch, but center fielder Casey Rowlett at least caused some Arkansas smiles with a two-out, phantom diving catch against Texas after the game was out of hand. It kept the Hogs from officially looking even worse. During the indecisive interim whether the two-out sinking liner was caught or not, Longhorns circled the bases like in a merry-go-round while Arkansas threw the ball all over Rosenblatt. The final errant heave landed in the first base dugout.

"Yeah, we knew he didn't catch it," Arkansas coach Dave Van Horn said, smiling about the ball's hop on the turf the umpire didn't see. "But it was a great play. He made it look good."

It kept the Hogs from officially looking even worse. As the Longhorns ran the bases like on a merry-go-round, they threw the ball all over Rosenblatt, finally into the first-base dugout, during the indecisive interim regarding whether the ball was deemed caught or not.

"I knew I'd trapped it," Rowlett said, "that it kind of one-hopped to me. But I just tried to get up and show it like I caught it. But I saw one umpire give the no-catch sign. So I threw it, and then all of a sudden I see the third-base umpire come over calling, 'Out! Out!' And I'm thinking, 'I'll take it.' Especially watching the ball get thrown around. It was a circus out there."

Calliope music would have been appropriate.

"I'm sitting there knowing the third base umpire called him out," Van Horn said. "And I'm watching the circus out there. The funny thing is the ball comes rolling into the dugout right by my foot. I'm the one who picked it up. And I thought, 'Wow, unbelievable!'"

Unbelievably Good

The unbelievably good far outweighed the bad, especially at Regionals with Arkansas, losing in the second round of the four-team double-elimination tournament to Wichita State Saturday afternoon after beating Le Moyne, coming back to beat Missouri Saturday night and then beating Wichita State twice on Sunday 11-9, 4-3 with Brady Toops's two-out, ninth-inning grand slam winning the afternoon game, and pitcher Charley Boyce throwing seven and two-thirds innings of winning relief in the nightcap after throwing six and two-thirds innings in a no-decision start in the Saturday Wichita State game that Arkansas eventually lost.

Junior catcher Toops achieved statewide celebrity status normally reserved for Razorback football and basketball players.

Wanna-be groupies, man-on-the-street recognition, e-mails from the unknown.

Nothing so startled him, though, as a particular comment.

"A person came to me," Toops said, "and asked, 'Am I looking at the guy who hit that grand slam?'

"I said, 'I guess.' I like to keep it low key, have people not know who I am."

Then he shouldn't have hit that grand slam.

"I know it," Toops said, laughing. "I don't know what I was thinking."

Brady Toops's two-out, ninth-inning grand slam against Wichita State in the 2004 NCAA Regionals was "the biggest hit of his life."

Actually, he knew well beforehand.

"I went up to the plate," Toops said right after the game, "thinking, 'This is what you live for. It is the biggest hit of my life.'"

Ironman Boyce

Arkansas coach Van Horn took some national flak for Charley Boyce throwing 203 pitches in two days at Regionals, but the third-year sophomore righthander, a business major with little realistic pro baseball aspirations because his fastball didn't get radar guns smoking, asserted getting Arkansas to Omaha was as good as it gets.

So as his Sunday relief stint against Wichita State kept increasing, Boyce became increasingly annoyed with Van Horn and pitching coach Dave Jorn asking if it was time to relieve him.

"We kept talking to him," Van Horn said, "and he said, 'Coach, quit talking. I'm not coming out!' And I think the players would probably have run us out of the dugout if we had taken him out."

A Dogpile Earned

Van Horn said if ever a team earned the SEC championship celebratory dogpile at Baum Stadium, this squad did, particularly after a Saturday night loss to Auburn made it do or die Sunday.

"We made the comment after Saturday's game," Van Horn said, "to meet at the mound, and they knew what we were talking about.

"They deserve it. When you are picked last and come in first in your league, that's huge."

The players never forgot where they were picked, especially while relishing a 15-3 final regular-season-day rout of Auburn that clinched the West by one game over runnerups LSU and Ole Miss and caught Georgia for the overall co-championship as the Bulldogs lost their final game to South Carolina.

"I like doing it 15-3," Jay Sawatski, the rubber-armed senior starter-reliever who beat Auburn twice in the three-game series. "It kind of proves there was no reason for us to be picked last."

Sawatski and the team liked it even more when Van Horn sported a postgame crewcut after the clinching victory.

"At the LSU Thursday practice," Van Horn said before the Hogs swept three from the preseason West favorite in Baton Rouge, "I said, 'We didn't come down here to win one game and feel good about it. We came down here to win the series and sweep!' After we won the first two games, some guys were talking about conference. And I said, 'We win the conference championship, I'll cut my hair like that.' After the Auburn game, they reminded me."

Hard to Shuck Cornhuskers

Nebraska didn't let go easily of Dave Van Horn, the Cornhuskers' coach of five years called home to Arkansas on June 21, 2002, to replace his retiring old coach, Norm DeBriyn.

Van Horn took Nebraska to the College World Series in 2001 and 2002, the lone times in their history the Cornhuskers went to Omaha for the national championship event, so the fans made a statewide effort to keep Van Horn from returning to his alma mater where he was an All-Southwest Conference second baseman for DeBriyn's 1982 Razorbacks and a graduate assistant coach on DeBriyn's staff from 1985-88.

"It made you pause and appreciate the people at Nebraska," Van Horn said. "I had two radio stations deliver more than 400 e-mails to me. One e-mail I got said, 'Arkansas ain't as good as it used to be. Signed, Norm DeBriyn.' That kind of loosened me up a little bit."

Even Harder to Shuck Cornhusker Media

O n the day and night he was trying quietly to tell Nebraska
athletic director Bill Byrne he was leaving and tell
Arkansas athletic director Frank Broyles he was coming, Van
Horn said he was stalked by the Nebraska media.

"The media was almost out of control back home," Van
Horn said the day he was hired at Arkansas. "Last night I had
reporters in my driveway at 9:50. I had to crawl around the
house so they wouldn't see us."

Donita Ritchie, Broyles's secretary, related that in one of
the many Van Horn calls to Fayetteville on his last day in
Lincoln, Nebraska a reporter came up to him and said apologet-
ically, "My editor said it's my job to go everywhere you go
today."

"You need to get another job," was Van Horn's reply
according to Donita.

The Nose Knows

A t his first press conference in Fayetteville, Van Horn talked
of his energy for the job and also that he had a bad cold
during the entire week that Arkansas and Nebraska locked in a
tug of war for his services.

"If you are this energetic with a cold," an Arkansas media
member gee-whizzed to the new coach, "what are you like without a cold?"

"The same," Van Horn replied deadpan, "only less nasal-
ly."

Chip Off the Old Block

In DeBriyn's 33 years coaching the Razorbacks, he put playing hard above all priorities for his teams. Ditto for Van Horn, who says DeBriyn by far has influenced him more than any coach.

"I always will promise our teams play hard," Van Horn said upon his Arkansas return. "If we don't, I'll be more than happy for you to tell me, and I will relay it to the team, and we will go from there. My goal is to host a Regional, host a Super Regional, with 7,000 to 10,000 people in the stands. And ultimately I want to win the national championship, not just once but many times."

The national championship hasn't been achieved, but the 7,000 to 10,000 in the stands are achieved and on the record.

Why Am I Here?

Like Admiral Stockdale, Ross Perot's running mate at the 1992 vice presidential debate, Dave Van Horn could have asked, "Why am I here?" when the eventual Razorback head baseball coach first came to Arkansas in 1982 as the second baseman for Norm DeBriyn's Razorbacks.

A Kansas City native, Van Horn was playing junior college ball in Waco, Texas, when DeBriyn, assistant coach Doug Clark, and the entire team were busing through for a Southwest Conference series.

"When I met Coach DeBriyn and the team," Van Horn said, "I was playing at McClennan Junior College, and I had already been on a couple of official visits to TCU, Baylor and A&M. When I got the call from Coach Clark they were coming that way, they set it up to meet them. At Waco they usually fed the team at a McDonald's there, so they said, 'Can you meet us there?'

"There were guys hanging out of the bus getting on the program, Coach DeBriyn was furious. I remember the players being kind of smart aleck. It wasn't one of Coach DeBriyn's favorite teams.

"I remember him saying, 'I can't believe you ended up here with that group.'

"And the first recruiting letter I got from Arkansas didn't say, 'Dear David.' It said, 'Dear Van' like my first name was Van. The outside of the envelope read, 'Van Horn.' Coach kept saying, 'Dear Van, how the hell did you end up coming here?' But this is where I wanted to come. It's amazing how things work out. I guess if I had been a highly recruited kid I would have said, 'They don't even know my name,' but it all worked out."

Making the Grade

Presumably, if you make good grades, you make the grade. At least that's what 2004 senior first baseman Haas Pratt presumed until he didn't see his scholarship renewal form starting the 2004 spring semester.

"Last spring academically Haas Pratt was in the mid 2s," Van Horn said in February of 2004, "something like 2.2 to 2.5. This fall semester he makes a 3.5. At semester we renew scholarships. Pratt hadn't gotten his in the mail. He's back about a week early over the semester break to work out and comes to one of the coaches and said, 'Did he take my scholarship away?'

"I told him, 'Hey, Haas, I thought you got an academic scholarship this semester!' But he did have his scholarship back and he is doing all right."

He certainly did, making the 2004 All-SEC Tournament and All-Regional Tourney teams.

A transfer from the University of Miami, Pratt had two good years as Arkansas's regular first baseman and went from the

2004 College World Series to being picked by the Oakland A's in the Major League draft.

Dugger and Hode

Freshman left fielder Jake Dugger and junior shortstop Scott Hode were pivotal for Dave Van Horn's 2004 SEC co-champion Razorbacks. However, while Van Horn applauded Dugger and Hode on the field, he's been bemused by the pair off the field.

"Dugger takes a lot of abuse," Van Horn said, "because he's always the one that's late or forgets something. He forgot his jersey before a road game Sunday. We figured it was at the hotel, but no. He could have sworn it was on the bus, 'I just have got to find the bus.' Well we check the bus, and it's at the hotel. I could go on and on about him."

What about Hode?

"Hode is Hode," Van Horn replied. "I wouldn't call him dingy, but it's close. Hode can't ask me any questions unless it's about signs or anything like that. Because he gets a little nervous, and every at-bat it's, 'How was this? How did I do? 'Finally before the whole team I just told him, 'No more questions. Don't ask me any more questions unless it's about a sign. But no how am I doing, or how about that? I'll tell you when I want to tell you something.' Now it's become a joke. Don't ask Coach any questions, Hode. But I'll tell you this, ever since we told him to stop asking questions, he's been wearing it out. Because he was nervous before, and now he's just playing. I took 18 hours of my masters in psychology so I'm using some of it. But on this team there really are no problems. They like each other, so it's been pretty smooth."

Part Four

Track and Field

Thanks a Bunch

While Razorback teammates handed flowers to the wives of coach John McDonnell and his assistants, Murray Link, the team captain and senior Canadian All-America distance runner, was at the podium publicly paying tribute to the wives at their 2001 track banquet.

"We appreciate the coaches," Link said earnestly. "But we don't appreciate their wives."

Murray froze in horror, wishing he could become a missing link.

"I'm not used to public speaking," Link stammered. "I'm just a dairy farmer from Canada. What I was trying to say was we appreciate the coaches, but we don't show enough appreciation for their wives."

Now Who Is the April Fool?

This April Fool's joke is on the *Arkansas Traveler*—some 60-plus years later.

According to the 1939 April Fool's edition of the *Traveler* that University of Arkansas emeritus information director Don Schaefer so thoughtfully provided, the Razorbacks' '39 outdoor track team was set to dominate the Penn Relays.

The '39 track team, during an era when the UA was strapped financially, was coached by football coach George Cole during his spare time. The UA track program forever, it seemed, labored under such low budget constraints, and consequently low ambition, that the UA student newspaper's April Fool's edition lampooned with this fabricated Cole quote: "I think that we will win easily, since all the important schools have dropped the Penn Relays because of our recent domination the past few years."

Who knew then that would come true for Arkansas with some teams dodging the Hogs at Penn to run elsewhere?

Since 1982, McDonnell's men have won all of Penn's relays, the 4x 100, 4x 200, 4x 400, 4x 800, 4 x mile, sprint medley, distance medley and shuttle hurdles, at least once and have won more relays and individual Penn titles than McDonnell can remember.

"It's got to be at least 50," McDonnell said. "Most of the time we average at least two a year. One year (1985) we won five relays there."

A Leprechaun Changes Track's Fortunes

'Tis fitting that a leprechaun launched John McDonnell's era from obscure surroundings to a path unprecedented.

Niall O'Shaughnessy, about as wee as they come at 5-6, 125, came out of Ireland as did McDonnell. The two from the Old Sod made for a distance running-coach combo that won McDonnell's first conference championship, the 1974 Southwest Conference Cross Country meet, and then drew national acclaim at the Millrose Games and other high-profile meets.

"Niall was a trail blazer," McDonnell said. "He was the high-profile guy who ran in Madison Square Garden and made the Olympic team. He was a lot like Mike Conley, not only a great athlete but a nice guy. Everybody that met him liked him. He'd treat the recruits that visited really well and made them want to come here."

Another Niall

O ther than being from Zambia instead of Ireland, Godfrey Siamusiye was Arkansas's Niall O'Shaughnessy of the 1990s in build, demeanor and success.

Siamusiye had been on nothing but national championship teams at Blinn Junior College, and he insured Arkansas wouldn't settle for less.

"He was great," Arkansas coach John McDonnell said. "His first year he told those freshman, 'I've never been on a losing team. And I'm not going up there to get second.' And those guys ran out of their minds. He was a special guy."

Not Quite a Leg Up

J ohn McDonnell recalled a runner he inherited who had more excuses than Heinz had pickles.

"This guy," McDonnell said, "one time said, 'I was leading by 10 yards and the guy tripped me.'

"I wonder just how long that leg was that tripped him," McDonnell mused.

He Ain't What He Am

O ne alleged athlete McDonnell encountered wasn't who he was supposed to be.

As head coach, McDonnell would coach some great African distance runners like Godfrey Siamusiye, James Karanu and Sharif Karie, but the first African-born Razorback he encountered was a sprinter named Peter recruited via mail and hearsay by his head coaching predecessor, Ed Renfrow.

Peter came with great track credentials—except they apparently weren't his.

They maybe were a cousin's, McDonnell guesses.

Peter, all five-foot-three of him, couldn't outrun a shotputter, much less a major college sprinter. He just wanted to get to the United States any way he could, though Fayetteville's January weather apparently wasn't what he anticipated.

"I remember going to his room to see if everything was okay when he got here," McDonnell, then the assistant coach, recalled. "He had the heat to about 90 and he had an overcoat on and was all bundled in blankets. All you could see were his eyes, and you could barely see them."

No one ever did see him in a race.

"One workout was enough," McDonnell said. "You could tell he'd never been on a track before."

Off the Wall

As a student assistant in the UA sports information department during the early 1980s, current J.C. Penney's executive Greg Fisher got assigned to track.

John McDonnell's program gave the rookie some rookie treatment for his debut, rooming him on road trips with some of the more—er—eccentric.

"One thing I will never forget," Fisher said, "was my first trip with the track team which was to Norman, Oklahoma. I can't remember the crazy shotputter's name who John had me room with one night. But I woke up about 3 a.m. to loud banging on the wall. And there, whatever his name was, was banging his head against the wall. I said, 'What are you doing?'

"He replied, 'I'm getting psyched for the meet!'

"I told John if he ever made me room with that nut again I would never travel with them again."

Row, Row, Row Your Boat

Irishman Frank O'Mara became one of John McDonnell's greatest Razorback distance runners, his first Razorback NCAA Outdoor 1,500-meter champion and an eventual member of the University of Arkansas Sports Hall of Honor.

But McDonnell didn't honor his fellow man from the Old Sod during O'Mara's freshman year. A bad leg by O'Mara cost Arkansas the distance medley relay to open the Southwest Conference Indoor Championships at Fort Worth.

"You run better or I'm putting you on the plane back to Ireland right now!" McDonnell fumed. "Forget the plane. You can row home!"

Move on, Harold

When Arkansas won its first SWC Outdoor Championship in 1982, McDonnell assumed Razorback David Barney would win the 3,000-meter steeplechase.

A Razorback walk-on, Harold Smith also was in the field. Maybe if the eighth and ninth runners both tripped, Harold could score, McDonnell figured.

"Harold's in second place," a graduate assistant told McDonnell early in the race.

"Ah," McDonnell said, "Get up there, Barney!"

Midway through the race, it was same scenario.

"Harold won't last," McDonnell said. "Come on now Barney! You're better than that. Pick it up! It's still yours!"

A lap and a half to go, and suddenly an Irish brogue filled the air.

"Move on, Harold! Move on!"

Harold did move on with a surprising second-place eight points that helped win the meet and won McDonnell's heart about as much any as any first place his elite athletes achieved.

Special Ed

Ed Williams, who became an excellent half-miler and part of the center of Arkansas's "Oreo Cookie" mile relay featuring Paul Jones, Bill DuPont, Williams and anchorman Stanley Redwine, used to be called Mr. Ed, because he did have a tendency to gab like the talking horse on the old Mr. Ed TV show.

Williams changed that name, for the worse he remembered.

During a four-lap indoor early-season meet 800-meters, the lap counter goofed and fired the gun on the third lap. Ed reflexively broke into his finishing kick, practically running the 200-meter lap like it was a 60-meter dash. Of course he ran out gas with still another lap to go.

"Can you not count?" McDonnell asked.

"Aw, you know me," Williams said, "Special Ed."

Ed laughed about it then and did again when he came back in 2004 for the reunion of the 1984 NCAA Indoor championship team.

In 2003, another Razorback, Michael Taylor, got caught up in the excitement and did the same thing on the distance medley relay mile anchor during the NCAA Indoor Championships.

Fortunately, for Mike, his name isn't Ed. Even more fortunately, Arkansas won that national championship meet.

Making a Splash

The first national wire photo encompassing a McDonnell-coached Razorback team wasn't what you might think. It wasn't a Penn Relays triumph or a national championship or a Mike Conley jump or Niall O'Shaughnessy or Joe Falcon breaking the tape.

"Our first national newspaper picture was at the Drake Relays," McDonnell said. "Tom Camien was running the steeplechase and fell into the water jump head first. I think it made every paper."

Arkansas did get to make sport of someone else's steeplechase misfortune.

Alabama's Tim Broe, who would win a SEC steeplechase crown during the interim between Razorback NCAA steeplechase champions Matt Kerr and unprecedented three-time NCAA steeplechase champion Daniel Lincoln, one time was giving heroic late race chase to Kerr when he ran too hard for his form and inadvertently plunged into the water jump at the SEC meet.

The next day's newspaper photos of Broe falling into the drink had all the Hogs snickering, "Roll, Tide."

McTrack over McSoccer

The world's greatest track coach once had no intention of running track, much less coaching it.

John McDonnell was gung-ho for soccer growing up in his native Ireland, and his brother, Frank, was the track guy until he asked John for a favor.

"He was training for a race," John said. "And he wanted to work on his speed. So he asked me to get a little head start so he'd have to run fast to catch me. He couldn't catch me, and I knew I had been in the wrong sport."

McDonnell became world class, once beating the great Jim Ryun, the best distance miler of his time.

Seeing Baseball in the Worst Way

McDonnell obviously never saw much baseball growing up in Ireland, but he learned about it in the worst way.

Always handy with tools and electronics, he taught shop at Greenland High School for his main income when he first was hired on at Arkansas as a part-time assistant to coach cross country and assist track coach Ed Renfrow in 1972.

Ten years earlier, McDonnell worked as a cameraman at WOR-TV in New York when he lived in the Big Apple while running track in the 1960s.

"It was 1962 and WOR carried the Mets," McDonnell said. "They were the worst baseball team ever (40-121 in their debut year). Not many saw more bad baseball than I did."

Texas Uptight

Texas never cottoned being supplanted by anybody in the Southwest Conference, but no group of Longhorns ever took it harder than the Longhorn track program when McDonnell won SWC triple crowns (league titles in cross country, indoor and outdoor track) from 1982-85 and 1988-91 before Arkansas abandoned the SWC for the SEC with a dozen national championships already achieved.

One year during a cold NCAA Outdoor Championship meet in Eugene, Oregon two members of Arkansas's qualifying 4 x100 relay team wore conventional shorts and two wore tights to keep their hamstrings warm during the prelims on a chilly day.

"Texas wasn't even running the 4 x 100," McDonnell said. "But they filed a protest saying Arkansas should be disqualified for running out of uniform. The appeals judge looked at me and said, 'Can you believe this ***?'

"The crowd up there started booing Texas, and they didn't uphold the protest."

Spontaneous Combustion

Arkansas hosted and won the 1985 Southwest Conference Outdoor Track and Field Championships as it simultaneously hosted and won the SWC Baseball Tournament at George Cole Field across the street from the track.

One of the track program's more poignant moments actually occurred at the old baseball field.

Saturday night, with the track meet already won, spontaneous applause started rippling then mushroomed to a crescendo during a lull in the baseball game.

The subject of the applause kept looking around to see what the fuss about until realizing it was about him. For all the accolades he would receive, John McDonnell never had a more spontaneous tribute.

Exceeding Expectations

Promoted by athletic director Frank Broyles from assistant track to head coach replacing Ed Renfrow in 1978, John McDonnell was not expected to win the 39 NCAA championships and 74 conference championships he's amassed, though as head cross country coach, his autumn Hogs had won the league meet from 1974-77.

"When Frank promoted me," McDonnell said, "I asked, 'What do you expect from me?'

"He said, 'Be in the upper half at conference.'

"I said, 'What about national championships?'

"He said, 'If we win a national championship once every 15 years, I'll be happy.' So I've got a lot of time left on my contract."

Long Drought

Hard to be believe, but the coach who has won 39 national championships once suffered from close-but-no-cigar syndrome.

"It looked for a while like I wasn't going to get one until '84," McDonnell said of when the Hogs won the NCAA Indoor in Syracuse. "We were second or third four or five times and I thought, 'I'm snakebit.' You hear about guys who go so far but can't win it. We thought we'd win it in '83 but SMU won it. I learned from that one. Frank O'Mara and Mike Conley both told me I put too much pressure on them. Guys have enough pressure besides thinking, 'I've got to do this. It's too much. I can't breathe.'"

Learn to Expect the Expected

"Later on," McDonnell said, "when we started winning, I never asked somebody to do something he hadn't done before. Now if you do something special, great, but if everybody does what they are capable of, that's a mark of guys with chemistry."

Out of the thousands of races McDonnell has witnessed, Alistair Cragg's virtual wire-to-wire victory over monster-kicking Michigan miler Nick Willis in the 2004 NCAA Indoor 3,000 may be McDonnell's favorite.

Coach McDonnell says that what Alistair Cragg has between his ears is what separates him from the pack.

The previous night, Cragg had won the 5,000 while Willis had spectacularly kicked down Arkansas's Michael Taylor on the mile anchor to win the distance medley relay for Michigan.

The 3,000 seemed an ideal test of Cragg's strength vs. Willis's speed, but Cragg had too much of both for the Wolverine to overcome.

"What he did to Willis," McDonnell said, "very few people could do that at that speed. He ran practically a four-minute-mile pace that last mile and a quarter. It takes a man to do that, I'll tell you. You can't realize how hard that he is. I always knew he had great qualities, but that 3,000 put it over the top. Willis is a very, very good runner, and Alistair just literally ran him into the ground. It took great nerve. He never wilted a bit. He just kept hammering and hammering and hammering, 60, 61-flat, with that guy right on his back all the way until the last turn. It took a lot of intestinal fortitude. He's not afraid of nothing. A lot of guys are good athletes, but it's what you have between your ears that counts."

An Irish Lesson

Scott Coleman was a rookie quarter-miler from Pine Bluff more than doing his part when he first heard the fabled Irish temper of Razorback coach John McDonnell.

The explosion occurred before a packed house and near a roomful of reporters interviewing Georgetown's victorious distance medley relay team at the Penn Relays.

Coleman asked sprint coach Stanley Redwine if a rookie could take early retirement.

"We were expected to win the DMR," Coleman said. "We had the same team, Robert Bradley, Eric Henry and Reuben Reina, that had won it the last year, except that I was running the quarter instead of Charles Williams, who had gone into the army. Before the meet, John gave everybody their race range of the performance he expected. I actually exceeded expectations, but the other three guys didn't. It was the first A-chewing I'd heard from him. I wasn't getting chewed out, but the other three were. Three All-Americans, three national champions, and I'm just a little peon that just got here. I told Redwine, 'I'm afraid to run again.' He just started laughing and said, 'You know John is Irish. You've got to expect that. Just do your job and don't worry about the others and you'll be OK.' And he was right. It was great running for John. But he has his expectations, and if you don't succeed, he'll let you know. Even if there's 40,000 people in the stands and there's a press conference going on."

A Steeplechasing Egghead

Comedian George Carlin used to give a sportscasting spoof announcing scores like "Boston College, 14, Notre Dame, 7; Texas, 21, Oklahoma, 17; Harvard, 24, MIT, 12 to the fourth power."

Daniel Lincoln can relate to that last score. Not only the greatest Razorback steeplechaser ever, but the most prolific NCAA steeple champ as the event's only three-time national champion at the NCAA outdoor meet, Lincoln graduated high school from the Arkansas School of Mathematics and Science in Hot Springs.

That school is not a track hotbed and didn't become one even with Lincoln's Razorback prowess.

"I don't even know if they know that I won," Lincoln said, smiling when asked about his high school alma mater after winning his first NCAA outdoor steeple title in 2001. "I haven't heard anything from anybody."

A Neglected Gem

A rkansas coach John McDonnell wishes he could claim credit for recruiting the steeplechasing great from such an unlikely source.

But he can't, even with Lincoln's parents living in Fayetteville at the time when he walked on with the Razorbacks only to graduate four years later as an honor graduate in biochemistry with a UA Medical School berth awaiting him once he puts aside his pro track spikes.

"He's the greatest story I've ever had," McDonnell said of going from walk-on to stardom. "And to think I never recruited him. He shows up with his mom and says he wants to come here. He recruited himself. I listened to other people who said, 'He's going to an Ivy League school. He's not going to Arkansas, blah, blah, blah.' And a lot of kids in Fayetteville in the past would go to a Tulane or some so-called big-name academic school. But Daniel is way smarter than any of those guys, and he chose here."

Lincoln not only won three NCAA steeplechase titles and one NCAA outdoor 10,000, joining hands with teammate Alistair Cragg, but twice won the SEC Outdoor Commissioner's Trophy as the meet's high point man with 30 for winning the steeplechase, 10,000 and 5,000.

"It still baffles me," Lincoln said. "If somebody asked me my freshman year if I would be a national champion, I would probably have said, 'No.' But that's all part of the ride, part of the excitement of doing things you didn't think you could do. That's why I am here."

Say, What?

Nobody came to Arkansas kinder and with more charitable intentions than the late Wallie Ingalls.

Wallie was the longtime radio voice of the Razorbacks and then the public address announcer for football games at Razorback Stadium and for home Razorback track meets and any charity event most anywhere. Wallie knew his sports, but as a public address announcer he was a by-the-book man.

If copy was presented him, or a name was listed on the program, he read it as is.

So when two Oral Roberts University runners leading a three-man 10,000-meter run were listed with names like Sharif Nbudzt and Ali El-Shahoud, Wallie read them as such, by gum.

This first perplexed then amused the ORU pair, both blonder than Madonna only, naturally so. Lars and Sven they might have been—but not Sharif and Ali.

Their heads swiveled each time they passed the press box. By the last mile they busted out laughing each lap.

Fallen Angel

As noted, Wallie Ingalls did know his sports.

Not so Johnny Angel, an announcer of sorts who worked briefly at Razorback events when the local cable operation's Open Channel would appear in mid-event to televise a Razorback track meet, baseball game, swim meet, etc.

Probing, Johnny's commentary was not.

Once at a track meet, Johnny surmised of a race: "Here they come ... there they go."

Geography wasn't a long suit, either.

Charlie Fiss, now with the Cotton Bowl but then a UA student assistant in the sports information office, couldn't resist playing tricks on Johnny Angel. Fiss told him 400-meter hurdler Charles Freeman of Dumas, Arkansas hailed from Sweden.

So, Johnny opined, "Well, you can tell he's from Sweden by the way his legs are muscled up. Obviously he's been running the Swedish Alps."

A Falcon Grounded

E ven after the rare defeats during his seven-time national championship Razorback track and cross country career, Joe Falcon never got a more blistering tongue lashing from coach John McDonnell's fabled Irish temper than he did debuting a cross-country winner as a freshman in 1983.

"It was the first meet we had lost in 77 races nonconference," Falcon said of the race the Hogs lost to Oklahoma at the Oklahoma State Jamboree in Stillwater. "I'm a freshman, and I went over and was going to run unattached and redshirt. When we got to the meet, we saw Oklahoma had a couple of Kenyan Olympians in on their team.

John saw what the teams were going to look like and he threw me a jersey. I'm like, 'What is this?'

"He says, 'If I have to tell you what that jersey is, you have no business running for Arkansas!' Then he started laughing and he said, 'You are going to run.'"

It was the last time McDonnell laughed that day, maybe that season, until Arkansas avenged the Oklahoma defeat in October and then went on and won its ninth straight Southwest Conference championship.

But back to this blistering September day that Falcon got blistered as a rookie out of Belton, Missouri.

"I'm like, 'Oh, my gosh!'" Falcon recalled. "I had never run five miles in a race before. I said, 'What do I need to do?' He said, 'Just stay behind the guys (Paul Donovan, Gary Taylor and David "Spanky" Swain were the aces at the time) as long as

Joe Falcon got a taste of Coach McDonnell's Irish temper for taking a walk in the park his freshman year.

you can, and when they take off just try and pick off a couple of Oklahoma guys.' I said, 'OK great!'

"The race is three o'clock in the afternoon in Oklahoma in a hayfield and it's about 100 degrees. Our great guys weren't going to kill themselves. So they take out pretty conservative. And the Oklahoma Kenyans were doing the same. At three and a half miles I was dying, but I was just at the back of the pack, when Spanky, Donovan and Gary along with the top three guys from Oklahoma tangled up going down a hill and they all fell. So I went sprinting.

"John sees us all going into the woods, and I'm up there just a little behind them, and then we come out of the woods and I'm in the lead. He's like, 'What the heck is going on?' He thought I had put on some huge move or something. Actually I'm dying, but I've got this lead going, and three-quarters of a mile to go there is one other guy from Oklahoma, and I take off and get away from him.

"With 20 meters to go I turn around. I can't believe I'm going to win my first race as a Razorback. So I stop, I'm wore out, and I walk the last five or 10 feet across the finish line. We hadn't run well, he knows we lost, so John immediately starts yelling at everyone to just sit down. He starts ripping everyone starting at the end of the pack, and he's going along and going along and I'm thinking to myself, 'He isn't going to be able to yell at me. I'm a freshman, I wasn't supposed to run, and it's my first race and now I've won.'

"When he got to me, he got madder than he'd been the whole time. He took his hat off and threw it down and took his clipboard and threw it down and said, 'If I ever see you walk across the finish line again with an Arkansas singlet on, you'll never run for me again! Do I make myself clear?' I was so scared that I couldn't say a word. I'll tell you one thing—I never walked again."

Gold Medal Faith

Had he been anywhere else in the U.S., Mike Conley would have had second thoughts.

But in Fayetteville at ceremonies on the Fayetteville Square honoring his winning Olympic triple jump, the former University of Arkansas nine-time NCAA triple jump and long-jump champion instinctively passed around his gold medal to the crowd.

"I looked at pictures of that the other day," Conley said as a United States Track and Field Association director attending the 2002 NCAA Outdoor meet in Baton Rouge, Louisiana. "That was a good experience. Being so close to everybody in a small town, it seemed like it was theirs, too. I never gave it a thought someone would steal it."

And nobody did, though some of Conley's former comrades in arms fretted.

"I was in law enforcement as a constable," Conley said. "So I had a lot of friends in police departments and they all joked with me about afterwards and said they followed it around. But I didn't think anybody came to the Square to steal the medal."

The Great, Bad and Bizarre

Dick Booth has coached the great, the bad and the bizarre during tenures from 1978-84 and 1988 through the present as the Razorbacks' field events coach and righthand man to coach John McDonnell.

"When we first got here," Booth said of 1978 after McDonnell had been head track for a year but cross country coach since 1972, "it was whatever Niall got and a couple of more points, and that was it. I remember how thrilled I was to get Danny Windler, because he had long-jumped 24 feet. He

Triple jumper-long jumper Mike Conley gave the Razorbacks something unique in the 1980s—a weapon in addition to distance runners.

jumped 24-9 at the Missouri Indoor, and I thought, 'What a stud!'"

Eventually, Booth would have long jumpers three and four feet beyond Windler's 24 feet including the still-existing all-time collegiate record 28-8 1-4 by Erick Walder in 1994.

That's the Pits

At least Windler, now a longtime medical technician in Fayetteville, always caused officials to break out the tape measure.

Officials left the measure in their pocket one ill-fated but sparkling clean triple jump in 1978 by Lake Village's Randy Brown.

The former Razorback is still a regular visitor and official at the Hogs' big indoor meets no matter where he has lived around the country.

"He laughs about that every time I see him," Booth said. "We were talking at the conference meet and somebody says, 'You know each other?' And Randy says, 'I might be the one he'll never forget. I didn't make the pit once. I came down hop, step and plop. I went 41 feet and it was 42 feet to the pit.'"

Take Your Best Shot

Booth coached some eccentrics in all the field events, but none more so than Scott Lofquist, a big-time shotputter who never seemed satisfied, no matter how big time he might throw.

"Lofquist almost intentionally fouled on the winning throw that beat Michael Carter (the eventual NCAA champion from SMU) at the Conference Indoor meet," Booth said. "I'm in the balcony at the Tarrant County Convention Center in Fort Worth, and he gets off a throw and he then starts having a fit, gyrating and shaking his head. He starts to step out the front of the ring (an automatic foul) and I holler, 'No!' He looks up, 'What do you mean, no?' I scream, 'Look at it, that's 66 feet!' And he says, 'Whoa, where did that come from?'"

A Fighting Chance

Lofquist and Marty Kobza were the best shotputters Booth coached, but 300-pound Gerry McEvoy, a former Irish policeman, was by far the most intimidating.

"He was an animal," Booth said. "One time he's in the weight room getting ready to lift and some football players are jacking around and he yells, 'Shut the %@# up!' And you don't hear a word. He was that kind of guy, from the wrong side of the tracks in Dublin where you had to fight your way everywhere."

Including maybe the field events coach, Booth once feared.

"He was by far the best thrower in Ireland, a high 50s thrower," Booth said of McEvoy in the 1970s, "but he gets over here, everyone is a 58- to 60-foot thrower and the pressure gets on him. That first meet he is as white as a ghost, and that first throw he's in the ring and just kind of pushes it. I couldn't go out on the track because the ushers wouldn't let me, so I'm on the edge of the stands and say, 'Gerry come here!' I take both hands and hit him right on the chest and say, 'What the hell is wrong with you? You look scared to death!' The red came right back in his face and he got mad at me. I'm thinking, 'I've just taken my life in my hands.' He says, 'I'm not afraid of anybody!' I go back up to the stands and the guy I had been sitting beside said, 'What happened?' And I said, 'It wasn't planned, but I just hit Gerry in the chest.' And he says, 'You hit Gerry in the chest?!'

"Well the meet is over, Gerry comes up to me and I'm thinking 'uh-oh.' He says, 'I really needed that.' He's still one of our program's great fans and lives and works in Fort Smith."

Champions All

Brown, McEvoy and Lofquist all got to be a part of the McDonnell era's first conference track championship, the 1979 Southwest Conference Indoor that stunned the Razorback staff.

"That first time we won the Indoor Conference," Booth said, "John and I weren't even keeping score. It was, 'That's a nice race, and Tony Kastl just won the high jump! Look at that!' We're nicking and knacking and finally it came down to the 4 x 400 relay, and Texas A&M had a real good one and is supposed to win the whole meet. They've got their trainer and a group of them set up on a corner underneath a corner of the banked track doing all those Aggie chants. Their runner is in Lane 6 and lost his balance and fell right into them—and we go, 'Just like an Aggie.' It cost them the meet. They are supposed to score 10 or eight points in the relay and they didn't get anything and we looked up and it's, 'We won?!'"

The Great Jumpers

Booth has coached top-flight athletes throughout the field events at Arkansas including NCAA-champion high jumpers Kenny Evans and Ray Doakes, but it's the horizontal jumpers who really made their mark, with Walder, Conley and

Robert Howard winning 28 NCAA long and triple jump championships just among themselves.

Add Edrick Floreal and Melvin Lister, five each, and Brian Wellman, two, and the Razorbacks have won 40 NCAA Indoor and Outdoor long and triple jump championships since Conley won the 1983 NCAA Indoor triple jump as a sophomore.

"A Mike Conley thing that jumps out at me," Booth said, "was the triple jump that year in Austin (the Hogs' first NCAA Outdoor title in 1985). "He was leading the triple jump and hoping he wouldn't have to jump anymore. It was hotter than heck, and he still had some running to do with with the 200-meter dash, and the kid from Tennessee had the jump of his life and took the lead.

"Mike was sitting back, leaning back on his hands underneath a makeshift weather cover. That guy hits the jump and carries on like he's won it and is jumping up and down, and I see Mike stretch and get ready and come down the runway and jump a foot farther than the Tennessee guy. He hits the sand, comes out and says, 'The guy made it too personal. There was nothing I could do but take care of it, no matter how I felt.' I felt that encapsulated how Mike was—that and that same night he's arguing with John about being on the mile relay. Mike's saying, 'You know I can outrun somebody on that mile relay,' and John says, 'Look, you've been in the 4 x 100, the 200, the long jump and the triple jump. If we can't win this thing without you doing everything, we don't deserve to win.'"

Walder Tops Them All

Because he wasn't as vocal as Conley and injuries severely hampered his post-collegiate career, Walder gets shorter shrift than deserved for the Razorback who won more NCAA championships than any other.

"He was kind of quiet," Booth said, "but Erick Walder arguably had the most impact. He won the most championships, he still has the longest collegiate long jump, and because there are three gold banners for triple crowns his sophomore, junior and senior years. He was scoring 20 points a meet for all of those. He was the Alistair Cragg (the Razorbacks' distance star of 2004) of that day, getting 20 points with very good people filling in around him."

Booth said the Hall of Fame display at Walton Arena, honoring Conley for a wind-aided Southwest Conference Outdoor winning 28-foot long jump in 1985 needs to be reconstructed to measure Conley's 1992 Olympic winning triple jump (a barely wind-aided 59 foot, seven and a half inches). Another display needs to measure Walder's 28-foot-and-a-quarter-inch collegiate long jump record to give both their proper due.

"Some day we'll get that figured out," Booth said. "Because it's not right."

Vaulting to the Presidency

Only one man has vaulted from the track team to president of the University of Arkansas.

Helena's Alan Sugg lettered for the late Ab Bidwill's track Razorbacks as a pole vaulter and eventually vaulted from there to the UA System's president's chair he occupies in Little Rock.

The goals were not simultaneous during Sugg's 1956-60 Razorback tenure.

"I was not thinking I would become president of the University of Arkansas when I was pole vaulting," Sugg said, laughing. " And I was always grateful that Ab Bidwill gave me a scholarship. I enjoyed being a Razorback. My only claim to fame as a pole vaulter was that I broke the University of

Arkansas pole vault record that had been in existence since 1929. George Streepy held it.

"It was 12 feet, nine inches. And when I was a freshman, I went 13 feet as a freshman. Freshman weren't allowed to compete for the varsity then. I won the freshman pole vault championship in the Southwest Conference. The highest I got later on was 14 feet. I wish I had done better, though 14 feet wasn't bad. It always placed at the conference. The best I ever got was second. I had the opportunity to see and compete in some of the nation's premier track meets such as the Texas, Drake, Penn and Kansas relays."

Of Lance and Wilt and Steel Poles

Sugg vaulted 14 feet pre-fiber-glass pole era.

"We were using Swedish steel poles," Sugg said. "Not much bend in those."

Sugg had a NFL Hall of Fame teammate on the track team and saw a College Football Hall of Famer become the Razorbacks' football coach during his pole-vaulting time.

"It was fun to be on the same track team with Lance Alworth," Sugg said. "He ran the sprints and was a great, great athlete. I was at the UA when Frank Broyles became head football coach. I remember all the football players were excited when Frank was named coach. They thought they had a winner and they did."

Sugg can also say he saw one of the greatest basketball players of all time win at track.

"I shall always remember seeing Wilt Chamberlain," Sugg said, "the tallest man I had ever seen in my life, win the high jump at the Kansas Relays."

Appreciating History

So many have athletes today have so little regard for history they wouldn't know to be honored like Shannon Sidney was when he met Clyde "Smackover" Scott.

One of the greatest athletes in UA history, Scott was an All-America running back for John Barnhill's 1946 Southwest Conference championship football team and was a champion SWC 120-yard hurdler and 1948 Olympic Games silver medalist.

Russellville's Sidney had nowhere near the UA career as Scott. Few did, But Shannon did play as a reserve wide receiver and special-teamer for Danny Ford's 1995 SEC West championship Razorback football team and in 1996 won the 400-meter hurdles for John McDonnell's Razorbacks at the SEC Outdoor Championships.

So Sidney and the legend shared a bond.

"I met Mr. Scott while I was getting an award," Sidney said of an award named for the late Bruce Mitchell, a Razorback defensive back in the 1970s. "It was interesting to meet him, pretty neat to shake the man's hand. Mr. Scott came up and introduced himself and I said, 'Take our picture!' I only got to spend five minutes with him, but it was really neat. If I was ever going to meet a Razorback from the past, I wanted to meet him. Forty-nine years later to have the same person who had done that congratulate me was cool. It put it all in perspective. You realize, 'Wow, that's Clyde Scott and he's telling me congratulations!'"

Winning for McDonnell

Winning that SEC 400-hurdles and an accompanying hug from coach John McDonnell always will be Sidney's biggest Razorback moment.

"It was amazing that I made the conference final," Sidney said. "Because I had tripped and fallen in prelims, but got up and managed to get the eighth spot. But I ran like I stole something in the final. I kicked it into another gear. I felt like I had finally pleased Coach McDonnell. I felt I finally accomplished something for him, that of all his champions, I was finally one of them and not second again. Feeling his hand on your neck when you win, that's not the average, 'Attaboy.'"

Eh, What's Up Doc?

Before owing what became an Olympic track career to running Razorback older brothers Randy and Rollie, and of course, Razorback track coach John McDonnell, Reuben Reina pays first homage to Bugs Bunny.

"I started getting involved in summer track in the third grade," Reuben said of following his brothers' track footsteps. "It came easy to me, because I used to run home every day from school in the second grade. It was about a mile, and I'd run home as fast as I could to catch the cartoons. I'd get there just in time to catch *Bugs Bunny*. As the Looney Tunes song would chime in, I'd always make it to catch *Bugs Bunny*."

Once Bugs Bunny got him hopping into track, Reuben kept going and going like the Energizer Bunny. Seven times he was a Razorback All-American in cross country, indoor and outdoor track and a two-time NCAA Indoor 3,000-meter champion and represented the U.S. in the 5,000 meters at the 1992 Olympics in Barcelona.

The Streak

Of all the remarkable achievements of the McDonnell era, Reina asserts the most remarkable is Arkansas annually winning a conference cross-country championship either in the Southwest Conference or SEC since 1974.

"Absolutely unbelievable," Reina said. "For all the things that could possibly go wrong... surely one of those years you are going to have guys sick, and we did. Joe Falcon was sick my sophomore year in Fayetteville and didn't even finish the race, but somehow we always had guys step up to fill the void. That's the tradition that's always been at Arkansas. When somebody is down, somebody steps up. That's what John says. You put on that Arkansas jersey, there's nothing expected but a victory. That's the rule, the way it is. Just putting on that jersey gives a lot of people that confidence that you are amongst the best and expected to be the best."

Circling the Wagons

As a Razorback freshman during the 1980s, David "Spanky" Swain remembers a victory circle circling into a ring of fire.

And it was he and his fellow Razorbacks getting toasted by cross-country coach John McDonnell.

"We had gone to Stillwater to the Oklahoma State Jamboree," Swain, an Englishman who continues to work and live in Fayetteville, said. "It was the third or fourth race of the season. Tommy Moloney and Tony Leonard were in the front pack, and Tony got kicked down and got second or third. But the team won and we're warming down and John stops us at the warm down and gets us in a big circle. And we're thinking he's going to say, 'Good job!' But he just starts winding himself up getting more and more upset. 'You all ran like dogs! By God, if we have a man up front, we ought to win the race! We ought to dominate!' He starts wearing us out and we're all confused.

"'Coach, we won the race.'"

Confused though they were, they weren't nearly so confused as Doug Williamson, the track team's sprint coach who had ridden over with the team to the cross-country meet.

"Here comes Doug Williamson," Swain recalled, "who was always a sort to clown around, He sees us all in a circle and he just thinks John is talking to us. He's completely oblivious to what's going on, and he runs up and just kind of staggers through this circle of guys and falls down and kind of does this dead ending in the middle of John's speech. Doug is lying on his back and he hears John giving us all kinds of hell and he realizes, 'This is not a good thing while we are getting our asses chewed out.' He just kind of crawled out from underneath it. And John never missed a beat. He just kept us chewing out."

Who knows? Williamson may have been ordered to flop through the circle just to test the team's concentration.

"It wasn't until about my junior year," Swain said, "that I realized John's speech was all planned. We were getting a little cocky. And that was John's way of centering us, not letting us get the big head. He does it every year. He'll pick some event somewhere two or three weeks into the cross-country season and lay the law down for the freshmen and sophomores who haven't figured it out yet. That's a key part to what makes John good. He wants guys to be quietly confident, but if he hears guys bragging and talking trash, he'll cut it out pretty damn quickly."

The Hog Who Stole Christmas

Now even under a disciplinarian like McDonnell, college kids are still college kids—especially celebrating a national championship.

Like when the Razorbacks won their first NCAA Cross Country title in 1984 in the cold on the Penn State campus at State College, Pennsylvania. They got out the team hotel for a Rolling Rock head start on holiday cheer that November night.

"We're out celebrating and drinking these bottles of Rolling Rock," Swain said of the Pennsylvania brewed beer. "We were out drunk, and it was the Monday before Thanksgiving and State College has got their Christmas decorations up. I decide it was woefully too early to have Christmas decorations up, and climbed up a lampost and pulled down one of these wreathes and stuff it in my jeans jacket and go staggering back. Somebody called the cops and Espen Borge (the Razorback runner from Norway) and I got stopped. They decide it's me they are going to arrest because of my footprints. I had climbed on top of a car to get to the lampost and they say, 'Let me see the soles of your shoes. Yep, they match.' I got carted off to the police station and they took me to some judge's house at two o'clock in the morning."

The Hog cavalry did ride to the rescue.

"Frank O'Mara rallies the guys," Swain said, "and they give up all their meal money to bail me out for $120. Some guy, I guess he was a judge, wakes up, I give him $120, sign a piece of paper and I'm home. You think about it now, and it was kind of a ripoff, but we sure didn't say that. We sobered up really quick."

Well, most of them did.

"Except Espen Borge," Swain said, "the quintessential Norse madman. He says, 'You've got my friend in a police car.' And he pushes some kid off a bicycle and wants to follow the police car on it. We get back to the hotel at six in the morning. We're all stumbling around and we're supposed to leave at 6:15 sharp and here comes John out of his room, 'All right boys, good job, you're up early! Let's go!'"

Of course they tried to act like they were feeling top of the morning rather than under the Rolling Rock.

"We have to drive a long way from State College to Pittsburgh," Swain said, "or somewhere like that to get a flight. That was the hardest journey we ever had in our lives."

Beating the NCAA a 39th Time

The 39th and most recent national championship the Razorbacks have won under track/cross country coach John McDonnell ranks among his most satisfying.

Not only did McDonnell's men beat the NCAA teams, they beat the NCAA itself.

At the NCAA Outdoor Regional meet, an unnecessary qualifying exercise that McDonnell and Lady Razorback coach Lance Harter both despise upon its inception two years ago replacing the simple system of qualifying on best performances, meet referee John Chaplin excused Razorback senior Alistair Cragg from the 5,000, Lady Razorback Veronica Campbell from the 100 and 200 and top Tennessee men's sprinter Sean Lambert from the 100 and 200.

All three would have run while injured. All three—two-time defending champ Cragg led the nation in the 5,000 and Campbell led the nation in the 200—were either at or near the top of their events.

Knowing it was an Olympic year and the risks of running injured went beyond the NCAA Outdoor Championships for the three elite athletes, Chaplin used common sense in advancing the trio to the NCAA Outdoor in Austin without them running those events at the Regional in Baton Rouge.

The NCAA committees, legendary for their lack of common sense, ruled Chaplin exceeded his authority. They deemed Cragg, Campbell and Lambert ineligible to run in Austin the events they didn't run in Baton Rouge.

Losing Cragg's automatic 10 first-place points in the 5,000 figured to jeopardize the Razorbacks' team title defense. Yet

Arkansas prevailed, 65 1-2 to 46 over runnerup Florida. Cragg won the 10,000, not run at Regionals, sprinter Tyson Gay won the 100, freshman sprinter Wallace Spearmon won the 200 and senior Chris Mulvaney won the 1,500.

For good measure, Lady Razorback LaShaunte'a Moore upset LSU favorite Muna Lee to win the 200 that Campbell would have been favored to win for Lance Harter's Lady Razorbacks.

"Afterwards," McDonnell said of accepting the team trophy, "some of the same people that kept Alistair and Campbell from competing were shaking my hand. After all the hullabaloo over the 5,000, it's nice to win."

Father and Son

Former Razorback sprinting great Wallace Spearmon Sr. and his son, freshman sprinter Wallace Spearmon Jr., of Fayetteville, had some family moments in Austin.

Spearmon Sr. anchored the Razorbacks to a 4 x 100 relay school record in 1985 that a quartet of Mike Thomas, Spearmon Jr., Gay and Omar Brown challenged but didn't quite match while winning their prelim in Austin.

Unfortunately, Brown got injured later that night running the 200. So it was a makeshift crew, with substitute Creighton Kiper sandwiched between Gay and anchorman Spearmon Jr., that didn't win like the first group might have, but still came home an All-America fifth.

The next night Spearmon Jr. did something his father never did, he won a national championship in the 200.

Did the son tell the father he had been one-upped?

"I'm not going to tell him that," Wallace Jr. said. "He's old, but he's still a little bigger than me."

Night of Atonement

Chris Mulvaney had won an NCAA Indoor mile in 2003, but two close-but-no-cigar NCAA Outdoor 1,500 runnerups in 2002 and 2003 compounded by a disastrous ninth-place nonscoring mile when he was favored in the 2004 really made it a do-or-die night for the English senior.

Mulvaney responded like a champ kicking down the field in the final 600 yards.

"After Indoors," Mulvaney said, "nobody worked harder than me. I wasn't going to throw away all that hard work. It's nice to finally get that first place. If I had lost by a half a second again, I would have been pretty gutted."

Alistair's Parting Shot

Of all the great Razorback distance runners McDonnell coached, Alistair Cragg is perhaps the greatest, McDonnell said, noting he's rivaled only by Joe Falcon.

Both won seven NCAA Outdoor titles, including a cross-country title by Falcon that Cragg never achieved.

However, Cragg easily could have exited with 10 national championships. He ran injured off nearly zero training while finishing second as a cross-country senior in 2003, handed senior teammate Daniel Lincoln the NCAA Outdoor 10,000 title when both joined hands crossing the finish line together way ahead of the field in Sacramento and then got victimized by the Regional officiating in 2004, depriving his quest for a third straight NCAA Outdoor 5,000.

That 13:16.98 Cragg ran at Stanford in April, 2004, not only led the nation and broke a school record, but met the Olympic A-standard making him an automatic selection for the Irish Olympic team.

"It's kind of funny," Cragg said wryly. "I can qualify for the Olympics, but I can't qualify for the NCAA."

Celebrate the Heroes of College Football
in These Other Releases from Sports Publishing!

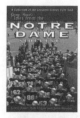